GOURMET TRAMPING

IN NEW ZEALAND

GOURMET TRAMPING IN NEW ZEALAND

John Sawyer and Liz Baker

ᑌᑭ

CANTERBURY UNIVERSITY PRESS

UNIVERSITY OF
CANTERBURY
Te Whare Wānanga o Waitaha
CHRISTCHURCH NEW ZEALAND

First published in 2007 by
CANTERBURY UNIVERSITY PRESS
University of Canterbury
Private Bag 4800, Christchurch
NEW ZEALAND
www.cup.canterbury.ac.nz

ISBN 978-877257-50-6

A catalogue record for this book is available from
the National Library of New Zealand

Edited by Rachel Scott

Design and pre-press production by Richard King

Printed in China through Bookbuilders

Contents

Acknowledgements

A number of people have helped in the writing and production of this book. We are very grateful to them all. Special thanks go to Jeremy Rolfe for providing images and designing the map and pan icon, Rob Suisted (www.naturespic.com) for providing images of the tramps, and Ross Brown, who took the superb food photographs.

We thank Marian Smith and Tony Dolphin for providing an inspirational spark by cooking brunch at Saxon Hut on the Heaphy in 1997. Jane Cooper shared her knowledge of wine and advised us on the best options for our tramps and meals. Karlene Hill, Chris White and Emma Riley provided many useful comments on earlier drafts of the book. We thank Rebecca Star for putting the two authors in touch with each other in the first place. Eamon Ganley, Dave Rogers, Dave King and Ed Steenbergen of the Department of Conservation provided helpful information about huts and tracks.

Images for the book came from a variety of sources. In addition to Jeremy Rolfe, Rob Suisted and Ross Brown, we would like to thank Greg Lind, Fred Wickham, Ken Scott, Eamon Ganley, Don Woodcock, Dave King, Heidi Meudt, Peter de Lange, Gillian Crowcroft, John Barkla, Owen Spearpoint, Rogan Colbourne, Ingrid Gruner, Les Molloy, Kelvin Lloyd, C. Rudge, Sonia Frimmel, Dave Crouchley, Keith Springer, Christopher Wilson, Maharani Allan, Carol Nanning, Tui de Roy, Marco Nef and Ferne Mackenzie.

We thank the wineries mentioned (especially Pegasus Bay, Crossroads, Cloudy Bay, Akarua and Matua Valley) for wine, sponsorship and permission to use their tasting notes. Without their help this project would have been far less enjoyable and our tramping less interesting.

Finally, we thank Rachel Scott and Richard King of Canterbury University Press for advice and encouragement, and for editing and inproving the manuscript.

Preface

Kia ora. This book is an introduction to the art of gourmet tramping. It takes you on a journey through some of New Zealand's most beautiful wilderness via some of the finest two-day tramps. Most importantly, it describes the fabulous food that you should take with you to complement your outdoor adventures.

Some people tramp because it is good exercise. A long walk in the bush cleanses the soul and teaches us a thing or two about ourselves. Others tramp because of the scenery and the wildlife . . . that sense of awe at seeing a flock of kea swirling like a halo over glaciers and lakes; the sight of brilliant white cascades plunging from black, scoured hillsides past prehistoric ferns into inkpot fiords. Others again (especially young Israeli men) tramp to get there quickly. When a sign says 'Four hours to next hut', you're a pansy if you can't do it in two.

For us, tramping is partially about exertion but mostly about indulgence, not only during the tramp (state-of-the-art tramping gear, extra-comfy walking boots, the latest range of Icebreaker clothing, gourmet scroggin), but also in the hut at the end of the day. So, having had our senses bombarded all day with views of unparalleled New Zealand landscapes, we treat our tastebuds to a delicious gourmet meal.

On trips when the view from the summit is less than breathtaking, gourmet trampers at least have the consolation of fine food and wine back at the hut.
Karlene Hill

Gourmet tramping has been around in New Zealand ever since Polynesians first colonised Aotearoa. In those days people fed on moa, coprosma berries, crayfish and kina. Since then the gourmet theme has been adopted by some hunters and tramping clubs, who regularly feast in the bush on all manner of wild foods. Nowadays, even at the most remote back-country huts you will find gourmet cooking of the highest standard, with young and old alike deliciously recouping kilojoules lost during the day's hike.

Imagine sitting in a hut of an evening with aromas of gently sautéed onion and garlic eclipsing the dank smell of

Food should be lightweight, fast cooking and high in energy value, e.g.

- Breakfast: cereal, firm bread, honey or other spreads
- Lunch: cracker biscuits, cheese, salami, margarine, jam/jelly, fruit
- Dinner: instant soup, pasta/rice, dried vegetables/fruit, cheese or dehydrated (freeze dry) meals.

You will also need: snacks, biscuits, muesli bars, tea/coffee, powdered fruit drink, emergency food in case of any delays on the track.

Your choice: the gourmet meals in this book or these suggestions from the Department of Conservation's guide to the Great Walks.

soggy tramping socks . . . On the table is a piping-hot plate of chicken with mushrooms and sun-dried cranberries. Then comes the sound of a cork being pulled from a bottle of Gibbston Valley Pinot Noir – or, even simpler, the slick twist of a screwtop . . .

But many trampers still find themselves at a hut eating sloppy, tasteless, uninspiring, reconstituted no-name dishes. These people have the enthusiasm for tramping but seem to be stuck for ideas for decent food at day's end. If the truth be known, they are probably fed up with ready-made vacuum-packed tramping meals, but have never considered that there is an alternative.

Does this sound like you? If so, this book will be more valuable to you than your insect repellent, earplugs and Lonely Planet's *Tramping in New Zealand* put together.

This book is all about sensory overload in the far-flung wilderness of New Zealand. We have never been fans of birdseed scroggin and energy bars, or the boil-in-the-bag 'just add hot water' instant pasta blarrrrgggh consumed by your average tramper. If, like us, you enjoy walking in the wilderness and cooking and eating truly scrumptious food, then this is the book for you.

Enjoy

John and Liz

Wellington
November 2006

Disclaimer
Although the authors have tried to make the information as accurate as possible, they accept no responsibility for any loss (losing your way in the bush), inconvenience (lack of good toilet facilities), injury (including sandfly bites), burnt offerings, inebriation, indigestion, food poisoning or allergic reaction (to ingredients) sustained by any person using this book.

About the tramps

You might think that gourmet tramping can be done any-where and anytime. Unfortunately this is not the case – the gourmet aspect involves carrying packs that are slightly heavier than usual. Unless you are extremely fit, therefore, you must choose your route carefully. We do not recommend climbing uphill for six hours carrying huge amounts of food and wine. If a local tells you a particular tramp is 'a bit of grunt', forget it and find another route.

As a rule, the perfect gourmet tramp involves no more than four hours' walking across relatively flat terrain. The tramps in this book almost all fit that description. They are all described as two-day tramps. The first day to tramp in, eat, drink and be merry, and the second day to head home – back to civilisation to recount tall tales of adventure and indulgence in the wilderness.

Some of these tramps form part of a longer route (for example, the Heaphy Hut is on the 82-kilometre Heaphy Track). In these cases you may, of course, wish to continue your journey. Some meals in this book can be eaten up to three days into a tramp, and these are noted.

We have deliberately excluded tramps on which food is available for purchase en route, as this reduces the incentive for you to cook your own. These include the Banks Penin-sula Walkway, the Queen Charlotte Walkway and the coastal route in the Abel Tasman National Park.

For each gourmet tramp we have included a range of information: the best time to go, how to get there, where to shop, and things to do near the hut. Most guidebooks advise you to tramp when there are as few fellow trampers as possible. Our advice is often exactly the opposite – a large crowd gives you an audience to mesmerise with your gourmet adventures. Tantalising them with delicious aromas may also inspire them to buy this book for themselves.

The notes accompaying these icons at the start of each trip description indicate the grade of the tramp, the best season to undertake the tramp, the time it should take, the number of bunks in the hut, whether or not gas is available and the relevant NZMS maps.

Great Barrier Island

1 Kairaara Hut

AUCKLAND

Thames

2 Pinnacles Hut

Rotorua

3 Sandy Bay Hut

Wairoa

North Egmont

4 Whakapapaiti Hut

Maketawa Hut **5**

Powell Hut

6

Masterton

Mount Arthur Hut

7

Heaphy Hut **8**

Nelson

9 Nydia Bay Hut

WELLINGTON

Westport

St Arnaud

10

Angelus Hut

Fox Glacier

CHRISTCHURCH

Welcome Flat Hut **11**

Makarora

Siberia Hut **12**

Queenstown

Te Anau

13

Luxmore Hut

DUNEDIN

Bluff

Mason Bay Hut **14** Stewart Island

Safe tramping

The tramps in this book have been graded using a simple set of criteria. 'Easy' means less than three hours' tramping on easy terrain. 'Moderate' means three to five hours, involving some climbing. 'Hard' means more than three hours with a lot of uphill slog.

Grades of tramps

The weather on any tramp in New Zealand can change at a moment's notice. Ensure you are equipped for all conditions, even if the forecast is for fine weather. Advice on clothing is included under 'Essential Tramping Equipment' (page 16). Accurate forecasts are often on display in Department of Conservation (DOC) visitor centres. National Radio broadcasts a long-range weather forecast at 12.30 p.m. each weekday, or visit www.doc.govt.nz for Metservice forecasts covering mountain and national park regions.

Weather

Be sure to fill in the intentions books before you set off on tramps – it could save your life. These books are usually found in huts, at visitor centres or at the start of a tramp. Remember also to sign out, if required, when you have finished the tramp so that no one wastes time trying to find you when you're not lost.

    Filling in an entry in the hut book is also a good idea – anyone that may be looking for you will know where you have been. It is also worth telling a friend where you intend to go and when you expect to return.

Intentions book

We recommend you take one but make sure you have it turned off when tramping to stop incoming calls destroying your wilderness experience. You may also need battery power in case of an emergency. Cellphones do not work in all back-country areas, so don't count on being able to use it.

Cellphones

There are rules about river crossing that very few people know about, other than a few keen boy scouts. One is that

River crossing

you should unfasten the belt on your pack before crossing a river. This is to prevent you falling over, banging your head, becoming unconscious and being subsequently drowned by your pack. Another rule is never to cross if you can hear boulders rolling along the stream bed.

Linking up with other members of your party – either by putting your arm through the gap between someone's pack and back or holding the shoulder straps of another pack – is the safest way to cross.

New Zealanders keep their boots on when crossing rivers. It is dangerous to walk barefoot and you will only slow everyone else in your group down if you stop at each river crossing and take your boots off to keep them dry.

If the river is high and you are in any doubt about making a crossing, wait until the water has abated.

Sunburn and hypothermia

'Wear sunscreen' is about the most useful advice anyone can give you for the ourdoors in New Zealand. Even on cloudy days this is advisable. We don't have deadly snakes and spiders, grizzly bears or yellow fever in New Zealand, but skin cancer through UV exposure is a greater killer.

Hypothermia is a life-threatening condition caused by prolonged exposure to temperatures below normal, and people become susceptible after a long patch of bad weather. Symptoms of severe hypothermia include being constantly cold, having depressed vital signs such as a slow pulse or respiration, slurred speech, a staggering gait, decreased mental skills and a lack of response to verbal or painful stimuli. Interestingly, sufferers don't usually shiver.

If you come across (or tramp with) someone who is exhibiting signs of hypothermia, then you must quickly prevent further heat loss. Insulate the person from the ground, protect them from the wind and remove any wet clothing (or cover them with a vapour barrier). Cover the head and the neck area to prevent heat loss and move the person to a warm place if possible, while awaiting transport to a doctor. Do not give alcohol.

Getting lost

It can be easy to lose your way if you wander off a marked track. If you do get lost on any of these tramps, don't worry.

Stay calm and be thankful you have gourmet food for your last supper. At least if you die it will be on a full stomach.

If you have a cellphone, and there is coverage, use it. Stay calm. Your emergency survival kit (see 'Essential Tramping Equipment') will undoubtedly contain copious amounts of chocolate. If you have filled in an intentions book, eventually the alarm will be raised and people will come to the rescue. Stay calm.

Water purification

The parasite *Giardia lamblia* exists in a number of New Zealand waterways and lakes, so we recommend purifying your water, at least for drinking and cleaning your teeth. This can be done by boiling it for at least three minutes, or by using a carbon filter. You can also use 2% iodine tincture or water-purification tablets, which are sold by tramping stores and chemists.

Rubbish

Carry out all your rubbish. There are no rubbish facilities on any of the tramps in this book – it is your responsibility to take out what you bring in. DOC provides good rubbish bags at visitor centres. Feel free to pick up any litter left behind by the slobs who were there before you.

Bush dunnies

Where it is provided, you should always use a hut toilet, however smelly it may be, rather than the bush. If no toilet is available, steer clear (at least 20 metres) of watercourses and dig a hole with the heel of your boot. Remember to cover after use. Do not go to the toilet beside the tracks. This is an unhygienic and disgusting habit of the lazy and mindless.

Flora and fauna

You will see many native plants and animals while tramping in New Zealand. Many are only found in New Zealand and some are extremely rare. Please do not disturb the wildlife unnecessarily. Don't take plants, however abundant they may appear to be. If you leave the marked walking tracks, minimise your disturbance of the vegetation. In alpine areas especially, it can take decades for plant communities to recover from trampling, so bear that in mind before heading off marked routes.

Essential tramping equipment

If you already think of yourself as a tramper, this list will be full of the obvious. It is included here as a reminder to those who have not tramped for a while and as a guide for tramping virgins. Because we assume gourmet trampers will use huts, the list does not include camping equipment.

Hut and track passes   To stay in any of the huts mentioned in this book you will need hut tickets. These can be bought at DOC visitor centres and some tramping stores. For tramps that are parts of a Great Walk (Kepler and Heaphy) you need to book to do the tramp as well. Booking must be made through DOC.

Pack / backpack / rucksack   There are good packs and bad packs. Make sure you have one that fits your back and is not so large that you cannot carry it full. Packs with wide and strong hip belts are good for transferring the weight to your hips rather than having it all fall on your shoulders. These days some packs have adjustable frames so that you can fit it to the shape of your back.

Pack-liner   In New Zealand a pack-liner is vital for keeping your equipment dry. They are available very cheaply from tramping shops, and all clothing and sleeping gear should be stored inside the liner when tramping.

Waterproof coat   A strong waterproof is essential for any tramp in New Zealand, not only to keep you dry but also to protect you from the wind. We recommend Macpac, Resolution or Hollyford coats.

Waterproof over-trousers   While it is generally warm during a New Zealand summer, when the wind blows and the rain is horizontal or turning to sleet and hail, a pair of over-trousers is very useful for keeping you dry and warm.

Tramping boots

The classic Italian-style hiking boot with Vibram sole is very good, but you can now buy excellent strong lightweight boots. The expensive ones are made with breathable Gortex material, but there are plenty of others to choose from.

Tramping clothes

Make sure you take plenty of layers and include a warm hat and gloves and longjohns or something similar. You cannot do much better than Icebreaker clothing, available from all good tramping and clothing stores. This is made from merino wool and comes in inner, mid and outer layers.

Some huts can be cold at night, and if it has been a wet tramp you'll want to change out of your soggy gear. Whatever clothes you take, make sure you have a spare set, including a long-sleeve top, trousers, dry socks, underwear and a warm jumper or fleece jacket. Again, the Icebreaker range of layered clothing is superb for wearing around the hut in the evening.

Wide-brimmed hat and sunscreen

In New Zealand we have clear air and very little ozone to shield us from the harmful UV rays of the sun. That means it's important to wear strong sunscreen (Factor 30). Covering up is a cheaper way of protecting your skin from the sun's rays. Many people favour baseball caps, but they don't protect the back of your neck.

Sunglasses

You can't put sunscreen on your eyes, but they too can be seriously damaged by UV, so sunglasses are a must. Don't bring the ones you got out of a Christmas cracker; use a pair advertised as having UV protection.

Insect repellent

Sandflies are actually supposed to be called black flies, but Captain Cook used the wrong word in his journal and the name stuck. The Maori had already called them namu. They are everywhere, and whatever you call them, they'll bite you regardless. There are two main species in New Zealand: *Austrosimulium australense* and *A. ungulatum*. The former is a problem in the North Island and along the coasts of the South Island; the latter is absent from the North Island but a serious pest in the South Island.

There are so many types of insect repellent available now

15

that it is hard to know which one to buy. We recommend the organic ones and those with less than 15 per cent DEET (the active ingredient). Some repellents contain 80 per cent DEET but, despite their being effective, we do not believe they are good for your skin. We recommend Aerogard Personal Insect Repellent (11 per cent DEET). Others are the chemical-free/organic repellents such as Native Spirit Insect Repellent and Sunblock, or Tui Bug Balme. All these can be quite effective. Sometimes it is easier to cover your skin by wearing long-sleeved shirts and long pants and socks.

Emergency survival kit A small kit with the following items (in no particular order) is a must: lots of chocolate, sharp knife, whistle, pencil/pen and paper, firelighters and matches, plastic bags.

First-aid kit This should contain at least: Plasters (big enough to cover large blisters on the heel), small nail scissors, a couple of bandages, antiseptic cream (such as Savlon), painkillers (with paracetamol), sore-throat tablets (such as Strepsils), antihistamine tablets/cream for stings, a needle for digging out splinters, and a roll of strong adhesive tape.

Emergency survival bag These huge (usually bright orange) plastic bags cost a few dollars from your local tramping or outdoor store. Learn how to use them before you leave home – few people know the correct way, which involves cutting a head hole in the closed end first. Instructions are written on the side of most bags.

Sleeping bag On most of these tramps in warm weather you would need only a light summer sleeping bag. However, for some of the high mountain tramps (Angelus, for example), or if you plan to do any of them in winter, you'll need a warmer bag. There's nothing worse than being cold at night, so it's worth spending money on a good sleeping bag.

Maps Most of the best tramps in New Zealand seem to be located on the junctions of four of the New Zealand 1:50,000 Map Series (NZMS). This must have been deliberately designed by the 'map people' to maximise the number of maps you must purchase. The description of each tramp in this book includes a reference to the relevant NZMS map/s. These are better than the DOC's own park maps, and can be bought at most good bookstores and at DOC visitor centres.

Rather than take the original map/s, we recommend you laminate a colour photocopy. This may cost more than the map itself, but it will save your maps from destruction by rain or from being constantly rammed into your pack.

If you are to carry one make sure you know a few basics – like which end points north.

Compass

Toilet paper is not always supplied at DOC toilets, so take your own.

An infinitely long toilet roll

These days many people use the small, quick-drying towels available from most tramping stores. These are very good but may not entirely cover you if you plan to use it them at the beach or lake.

Towel

Each person needs an unbreakable plate or bowl, a mug and a set of cutlery. Some trampers eat out of the cooking pots, but gourmet trampers don't. Presentation is all important.

Plate or bowl, mug and cutlery

Many trampers wash their dishes when they get home, but it's sometimes better to clean up after the meal.

Teatowel, pot scrubber and washing-up liquid

The best tramping torch is the Petzl head torch, although you tend to look like a coalminer when walking around the hut at night. They cost a little more than your standard torch (as do the batteries), but are a valuable asset. Carry a spare bulb and batteries.

Torch

Whether you are in a romantic mood or not, candles add that extra bit of atmosphere to a hut dinner. They're also very useful when you lose your torch or realise you have forgotten the spare batteries.

Candles

The obvious choice is the range of Victorinox Swiss Army knives, though you can now buy cheaper brands that are almost as good.

Pocketknife

Water bottle Most people now seem to use CamelBaks or Platypus water carriers. These are plastic water-holders that you stash on the side of your pack, with a long tube so you can drink without having to take your pack off. Plastic or aluminium tramping bottles work just as well. They should hold at least one litre.

Waterproof matches Waterproof matches are now so cheap they are a much better option than trying to keep your ordinary matches dry. Tramping stores sell them.

Pen/pencil and paper Just in case you are overcome by the urge to write poetry, or need to score when playing cards, or want to play noughts and crosses.

Camera Make sure you charge the batteries (and remember to take them out of the charger) before leaving home.

Binoculars Always useful for identifying those elusive forest birds or interesting flora.

Plant and bird identification books Andrew Crowe's *Which Native Forest Plant?* is very good, and light to carry. *Which Bird?* by Andrew Crowe and Dave Gunson is useful for bird identification. Gerard Hutching's *The Natural World of New Zealand* is a good read before you go but it's a hefty tome you would probably not take on a gourmet tramp (especially if it meant leaving the wine behind).

Cards and games Whether you are into strip poker or just straight bridge or rummy, a pack of cards is one of the easiest ways to amuse yourself and others in the hut. Few people think to take games tramping, but Twister has to be one of the lightest to carry and great fun for a group.

Gourmet tramping gear

Every chef has his or her own essential equipment. You can't take it all tramping, but listed below are what we consider the 'must have' utensils for gourmet tramping chefs.

Portable stove and fuel

There are many different types of stove to choose from. Multi-fuel stoves (MSR) are probably the most popular, although gas burners (with small canisters) and Trangias (using methylated spirits) are also very good. Some huts in this book have gas cookers with gas supplied, but it is wise to carry your own just in case. (A gourmet tramper does not want to be caught with no cooking facilities.)

Note that gas canisters and fuel bottles are not permitted to be taken on aeroplanes, so you'll need to remember to buy them at your arrival point.

Frying pan

MorganWare is the finest cookware ever made, as the manufacturer will tell you, and we agree. The non-stick stainless-steel omelette pan is perfect for cooking all the meals in this book. Take the lid with you, even if it means extra weight, as it is good for keeping your food warm. The pan is also very easy to clean and not too heavy.

Cooking pots

We recommend the LOOK Cookware 1.5-litre pot or something similar, and a smaller pan. Or you can take a large tramping billy with a set of smaller ones. MSR aluminium pots are also a good option.

Wooden spoon

Never leave home without one.

Sharp knife

We like the Victorinox 11-centimetre Tomato and Sausage Knife with wavy edge. These come in red, blue or black.

Our knife of choice from the Victorinox range.

Film cannisters and medicine bottles are perfect for carrying small but essential ingeredients.

Bottle opener   You probably have one of these on your Swiss Army knife.

Small screw-top dispensing bottles   These can be bought very cheaply from most pharmacies and make great containers for olive oil, balsamic vinegar and washing-up liquid. They come in several sizes and you cannot have enough of them. Buy the ones with childproof lids. It is sensible to label them so you don't end up frying your blue cod in detergent.

Film canisters   These are perfect for carrying herbs and spices.

Salt and pepper container   Bivouac's Rocco container is great, but there are plenty of others available. You should add a few rice grains to keep the salt dry.

Nail scissors   These are very useful for cutting fresh herbs and opening packets. You should have a pair in your first-aid kit, but a spare one in your kitchen equipment is also useful.

Coffee plunger   Some gourmet trampers would not be able to survive without real coffee. Some shops sell plastic tramping mugs with a built-in plunger.

Serving plate   One of these adds a classy touch when serving your meal, but probably best not to take Nana's heirloom platter.

Wine and food matching

The wines chosen to accompany the meals in this book are from only seven of New Zealand's 19 wine regions: Gisborne, Hawke's Bay, Martinborough, Marlborough, Nelson, Waipara and Central Otago. There are now over 400 wineries in New Zealand and we have selected wine from only 28 of those.

For each meal we have named our preferred option and up to three alternatives. Each is selected either because it comes from a winery in the vicinity of the tramp or because it goes perfectly with the meal. However, our taste might not be the same as yours, so feel free to experiment with others. A good way to do this is to take a wine trail in whichever region you are in and taste a few of the local wines.

When matching food with wine, try to think about the predominant flavours in the meal, and match these with typical flavours you might find in a particular type of wine. For example, chicken with sun-dried cranberries and mushrooms will probably emphasise the cranberry and mushroom flavours. When we look at grape varieties, the wine most likely to show these flavours would be pinot noir.

Try also to match the strength of the flavours in the meal with the strength of flavour of a wine. This can be a little more difficult if you haven't tried the wine, but you can generalise about some varieties and say that, for instance, most chardonnays (except the unoaked ones) tend to be quite strongly flavoured and even rich, so that you will need a strongly flavoured dish to go with it.

A poor match is one where either the food drowns out the flavour of the wine or vice versa.

Hot spicy food is hard to match with wine, and it may be best on these occasions to opt for your favourite beer.

When eating desserts, it is probably best to switch to a bottle of botrytis or dessert-style wine where the sweetness levels will be similar. Drinking a big pinot or chardonnay with a main meal can taste great, but the wine doesn't often seem as good when you start eating something sweet.

Other alcohol options A six-pack of beer is good for the happy hour if you can be bothered carrying them. We recommend Monteith's because the bottles always look good in a hut. A small plastic bottle of Pimm's and a couple of bottles of lemonade to mix with it never go amiss. Add some mint leaves or chopped cucumber. A hip flask or an old water bottle filled with your favourite whisky is very good to round things off as you sit on the deck of the hut discussing the meaning of life.

Mulled wine Another option (especially during the colder months) is to prepare a billy of heart-warming mulled wine.

750 ml red wine (any)
a few splashes of brandy (doesn't have to be flash)
2–3 cinnamon sticks (or 1 tsp ground)
4–5 whole cloves (or ½ tsp ground)
rind and/or juice of an orange (use a potato peeler)
approx. 1 tbsp sugar (according to taste)

Heat all the ingredients together in a pot for long enough to dissolve the sugar, but don't let the mixture boil – this will cause the alcohol to evaporate.

Kick off your gourmet evening with a mug of mulled wine.
John Sawyer

Transporting your produce

The age-old problem of taking fresh meat or fish on a tramp can be solved in several ways. To start with, keep all your meat, fish and dairy products refrigerated until the last minute. If you are driving to your destination, transfer these items to a chilly-bin for the journey.

If you intend to shop immediately before starting the tramp, ask the vendor to place the meat or fish in a bag with some ice. Then wrap the bag in newspaper to keep it cool for your tramp.

A good option is to freeze the meat overnight before you leave, then carry them in a sealed plastic bag wrapped in newspaper. Bury the parcel deep in your pack to keep it cool. However, most of these tramps are short enough that it will be fine to carry fresh meat, wrapped well. If you are marinating the meat (e.g. for the Moroccan Beef), put in a sealed plastic bag with the spices before you set off.

Bacon

Bacon in a sealed packet will survive for several hours. Remember to keep it in the fridge until you set off.

Blue cod

This is bought locally on Stewart Island so should be very fresh. Wrap in a sealed plastic bag and then newspaper and it will be fine after a few hours' tramping.

Hot smoked salmon

Again, buy this in a sealed pack and keep it in the fridge until you leave home.

Salmon

Wrap the fillets in plastic, then in newspaper and put the parcel in a well-sealed plastic container, preferably with ice.

Eggs

You can either crack the eggs into a sealable tub (e.g. a recycled supermarket pesto tub), or you can cut the portion you need out of an egg carton, place the eggs in it, wrap in tissue paper and put it in a box or small billy.

'Must have' ingredients

The recipes in this book are designed to cater for two hungry trampers. The 'must have' ingredients for all tramps, gourmet or otherwise, are:

- salt and pepper
- milk powder
- olive oil
- tea bags
- sugar
- garlic
- onions.

No tramp is complete without a cup of tea. Shefali Roy, John Sawyer and Chris White toast their arrival at a hut and prepare themslves for the rigours of Happy Hour.

John Sawyer

Breakfasts, lunches, snacks

We have not specified a particular breakfast for each tramp. Here are a selection from which you can choose, depending on the time of year and your personal preferences. We recommend taking a litre container or carton of freshly squeezed orange juice to add a touch of class to any breakfast.

Light breakfasts

If you're not used to a big breakfast, you'll still need fuel for your body to burn as you tramp out. Here are a few light breakfast options.

Gourmet muesli

½ cup wholegrain oats
¼ cup oatbran
¼ cup wheatgerm
(Mix the above ingredients together before you leave)
1 cup fresh orange juice
juice of 1 lemon
1 mashed banana or 1 grated apple
1 cup natural yoghurt
2 tbsp liquid honey
½ cup mixed dried fruit, nuts and seeds

Soak the grains overnight in the orange and lemon juice. In the morning, mix in banana or apple, yoghurt and honey. Divide into 2 bowls and top each with ¼ cup of dried fruit, nuts and seeds.

Grapefruit

The simplest breakfast of all, and one of the most delicious, is a grapefruit or two. Cut them in half and sprinkle sugar and/ or cinnamon on top if desired.

Gourmet porridge

This traditional tramping breakfast is a divinely decadent way to start the day when served with cream and brown sugar.

3 cups milk
pinch of salt

A great start to the day: gourmet porridge and a cuppa.
John Sawyer

1½ cups rolled oats
chopped dried apricots or prunes (soaked overnight) or dried
    cranberries and chopped almonds (roasted or not)
cream
brown sugar

Pour the milk into a pot, add the salt and heat gently. After a couple of minutes add the rolled oats and stir. Keep stirring until the porridge starts to thicken, and bring it to a light boil. If it still looks a bit runny, add more oats (or more milk if too thick). Add fruit or nuts if desired. Pour into 2 bowls and add cream. Sprinkle brown sugar over the top with.

As a variation, chop an apple into the porridge and sprinkle cinnamon over the top.

Serious breakfasts If you need building up for the return tramp, we recommend one of the following more substantial breakfasts.

Bacon and avocado bagels 250 g honey streaky bacon
olive oil
butter
2 bagels
1 avocado
1 tomato
salt and pepper to taste

Fry the bacon gently in the olive oil. Cut the bagels in half and butter both sides. Slice the avocado and tomato and arrange on the bagel bottoms. Top with bacon and season.

Pancakes with bacon, banana and maple syrup

200 g plain flour
2 eggs
pinch of salt
2 cups milk
1 banana
200 g bacon
juice of 1 lemon
maple syrup

Place the flour in a bowl and break in the eggs. Stir. Add the salt and stir again. Add the milk a spoonful at a time, stirring after each addition until the milk is fully absorbed. Keep adding the milk until the batter is a good consistency: not as runny as water but not so thick a spoon can stand up in it. Mash the banana and add it to the batter. Stir.

Assuming you have only one frying pan, fry the bacon before you cook the pancakes and keep the rashers warm in a covered bowl.

Heat the frying pan and pour in enough batter mixture to just cover the bottom of the pan. Cook until the top is no longer liquid and/or the bottom of the pancake is brown (2–3 minutes). Turn the pancake over and cook for a further 2 minutes.

Serve the pancakes with the bacon on top and with a squeeze of lemon juice and maple syrup.

Author John Sawyer making pancakes for breakfast.
Stephanie Arlaud

Gourmet fry-up

The traditional fry-up may seem obvious, but few realise how easy this is to cook on a tramp. The smell of frying bacon will drive your fellow trampers crazy as they struggle with burnt toast and instant coffee.

2 tbsp olive oil (for frying)
4 sausages (preferable gourmet variety)
4 rashers of bacon
2 tomatoes, halved
2 large flat brown mushrooms
2 eggs

small loaf of ciabatta
butter

Fry the sausages for several minutes (depending on their thickness) in half the oil. Add the bacon to the pan and continue to cook. After a couple of minutes add the tomato halves (cut side down), followed by the mushrooms (sliced if you like). When everything is cooked, pile it into a covered pot to keep warm.

Fry the eggs to your liking in the remaining oil and serve all together with buttered ciabatta.

Vegetarian gourmet fry-up

1 tbsp olive oil (for frying)
2 eggs
2 croissants
200 g haloumi cheese (4 slices)
25 g rocket
6 large brown flat mushrooms, sliced
1 avocado, sliced
1 tomato, sliced
salt and pepper to taste

Fry the eggs and set aside. Fry the mushrooms for 2 minutes, add the haloumi cheese to the pan and fry lightly for a further 4 minutes.

Cut the croissants in half horizontally and dress the bottom halves with the rocket, avocado and tomato. Place the eggs, cheese and mushrooms on top and season if desired.

Gourmet lunches and snacks

It is important that you stay hydrated and keep your energy levels up during the tramp. Most people have strong preferences for their lunches and tramping snacks. A few ideas are provided here, or you may prefer to munch on scroggin or muesli bars and save yourself for the evening meal.

Antipasto selection

Most people have their own favourite cheeses, meats and olives. The following are just some that would make a lunch stop an absolute treat. Pack some tortilla wraps or crackers (e.g. Vitawheat, Ryvita or water crackers) to eat with it.
• Kapiti Triple Blue cheese

A simple selection of antipasto lunch ingredients.
John Sawyer

- olives (Chilean or Kalamata)
- Blackball smoked venison salami
- cherry tomatoes
- chargrilled peppers
- basil pesto

Smoked salmon and cream cheese bagels

2 plain bagels
small tub of cream cheese
200 g salmon pieces
leafy greens

Pile the ingredients into halved bagels and enjoy.

Soup with ficelle

Most supermarkets stock an array of tasty, ready-made soups, such as carrot and coriander or spicy tomato. Heat the soup before you leave civilisation and carry it in a Thermos. Serve in a mug with a buttered ficelle bread.

Another option is taking sachets of miso soup, which just need hot water added.

Gourmet scroggin

Scroggin is a Kiwi tramping tradition. The name comes from the first initials of the traditional ingredients (sultanas, chocolate, raisins, orange peel, ginger, glucose, imagination and nuts). The 'imagination' ingredient allows you to customise your scroggin.

New Zealand supermarkets sell a good standard mix (usually in the bulk-buy bins), which, when supplemented with a few choice additional ingredients, can be delicious. However, we believe the perfect scroggin requires some changes to the acronym. Try the following recipe for gourmet scroggin – the finest you'll taste either side of the dateline!

- chocolate-covered almonds
- prunes and dried apples
- pumpkin seeds
- brazil nuts
- lumps of your favourite chocolate
- dried apricots
- raisins

Dessert and coffee

There are several options for gourmet puddings, from the full-on plateful to a light sweet treat with coffee. Either way, you can justify it after that hard slog to the hut and the knowledge that you need building up to hike out the next day.

Full-on gourmet puddings

There are several options here, depending on how hungry or decadent you feel. A packet cheesecake can be spruced up with a few fresh strawberries. Here are some other options.

Aunt Betty's steamed pudding with custard or cream

2 individual Aunt Betty's steam puddings
1 small bottle of cream
or
3 tbsp milk powder
2 cups water
2 tbsp custard powder
2 tsp sugar

This is an easy option but delicious and filling. Make sure you have enough fuel in your stove as boiling the puddings takes 15 minutes. Cook the steam puddings as per instructions on packet. Serve with cream.

Alternatively, make custard by mixing the milk powder thoroughly with the water, then heat gently. After a couple of minutes add the custard powder and sugar and continue to heat, stirring all the time, until the mixture thickens.

1 punnet strawberries
1 banana
½ melon (save the other half for breakfast)
2 kiwifruit
1 small bottle of cream

Fruit salad with cream

Chop up the strawberries, banana and the half melon into a bowl. Peel, slice and add the kiwifruit. Mix gently. Whip the cream with a fork or a small hand whisk serve over the fruit.

4 rhubarb stems cut into 10 cm lengths
2 tbsp sugar
1 lemongrass stem, lightly crushed to release the flavour
a few pieces of crystallised ginger, finely chopped
1 clove
2 tbsp water
1 small bottle of cream
biscotti

Stewed rhubarb and cream

Put all the ingredients (apart from the cream and biscotti) in a pot. Bring to the boil, cover and simmer for just a few minutes until tender. Serve with whipped cream and biscotti.

It is always nice to have a packet of crackers and a block of your favourite cheese (double-cream camembert is one of ours). These are good for an after-dinner snack or as part of your pre-dinner happy hour.

Cheese and crackers

Whatever your favourite chocolate may be, bring lots. There are some obvious choices. The Seriously Good Chocolate Company from Invercargill is aptly named and their products are widely available. There is a huge range of other chocolate out there, so you are spoilt for choice.

Chocolate

If you take a tramping coffee plunger and some ground coffee, pack a couple of miniatures of Baileys Irish Cream or a similar tipple to add to it.

Sweet treat with coffee

Chocolate brownie travels well and is the perfect coffee accompaniment. If you want to make your own brownie before you leave, here's our tried and trusted recipe:

Chocolate brownie

2 eggs
2 tbsp milk
1 tsp vanilla essence
225 g sugar
100 g self-raising flour
35 g cocoa powder
pinch of salt
125 g margarine or butter, melted
50 g chopped walnuts

Beat together the eggs, milk and vanilla. Add this to a bowl containing the sugar, flour, cocoa and salt. Stir in the melted margarine or butter and walnuts. Pour into a greased sandwich tin and bake at 160°C for about 25 minutes.

Chocolate brownie – sweet as!
John Sawyer

Kaiaraara Hut
Great Barrier Island/Aotea

Great Barrier Island is about 90 kilometres northeast of Auckland in the outer Hauraki Gulf, and the largest North Island offshore island. Its English name, given by Captain Cook in 1769, refers to the protection this island provides to the Hauraki Gulf. Its Maori name, Aotea, means 'land like a white cloud'.

About 1,300 people live there, although over 60 per cent of the island is administered by DOC. The island is a sanctuary for rare native species such as the brown teal, the black petrel and Great Barrier Island kanuka.

2 hours   30 bunks   No

Easy

Spring, late summer–autumn

NZMS 260 S8 Barrier

Time required
Two hours is all you will need to reach the hut, with a further two if you want to walk up the Kaiaraara Valley to the kauri dams.

The best time to go
The weather on Great Barrier Island is usually good year round, so this tramp can be done at any time. Spring (October and November), late summer and autumn (mid-February to April) are the best times to visit if you want to avoid the holiday peak of late December–January. After heavy rain it can be difficult to cross the Kaiaraara Stream, which you have to do several times during the tramp, so watch the weather before you head off.

Olearia allomii, a tree daisy endemic to Great Barrier Island.
GILLIAN CROWCROFT

Getting there
The quickest – and most scenic – way to get to Great Barrier Island is to fly to Claris or Okiwi. Flights leave from the North Shore and Auckland airport at Mangere, and take about 30 minutes. Out-of-towners need to know that the drive to Auckland airport can be a nightmare, so you should allow plenty of time. We recommend that you pre-book a

Kaka are abundant on Great Barrier Island and can be heard screeching as they fly overhead.

John Sawyer

Kauri dam, Kaiaraara Valley.

Rob Suisted

taxi or shuttle to take you from Okiwi to Port Fitzroy (Mike Newman Transport is a good option.)

In mid-summer Fullers run catamarans from the harbour in downtown Auckland to Tryphena and then on to Port Fitzroy. For the rest of the year Sealink operate a service leaving from Wynyard Wharf on Tuesdays at 7 a.m. but will not drop you at Port Fitzroy until 4 p.m.

The shopping

We recommend you buy your supplies (including wine) in Auckland. There is limited shopping on Great Barrier Island but you will pay a lot more. There is a small grocery store at Port Fitzroy and you can buy alcohol there if you forget anything or you want to support the local economy. Cooking fuel, including methylated spirits but not necessarily gas, is also available at this store.

The tramp

This tramp is not the most spectacular of the walks described in this book, but it is interesting and beautiful and well worthwhile. From Port Fitzroy, walk south along the Kaiaraara Bay Road. This climbs above the coast with views over Rarohara Bay. Watch out for the numerous kaka that screech loudly and fly around Port Fitzroy.

After about 20 minutes you'll come to the DOC office, where you can buy your hut tickets. The road continues to climb and crosses over the headland that separates Rarohara and Kaiaraara Bays.

When you pass the locked gate at the end of Kaiaraara Bay Road you are entering the Great Barrier Forest. From here the road descends to the Kaiaraara Stream, which you then ford several times. Normally this is easy, but after heavy rain you may have to turn back. After crossing the stream the first time you will see an information sign and map. Continue to follow the road, which fords the stream a couple more times before you arrive at the hut.

For fit trampers who do not mind a harder day's walk, we recommend flying to Claris and catching the People and Post bus (departs at 10 a.m.) to Windy Canyon. The five-hour walk up and over Hirakimata (Mt Hobson) through regenerating

kauri forest is spectacular. This tramp can be tough on the legs when descending and it is treacherous in wet weather.

Below Mt Hobson/Hirakimata on the Kaiaraara track.
Rob Suisted

The hut

Kaiaraara Hut sleeps 30 people on sleeping platforms and is surrounded by kanuka and regenerating forest. There are two bunkrooms of equal size, and the kitchen in the centre of the hut has a woodburner. Places in the hut cannot be booked – it is first come, first served.

Things to do nearby

A two-hour side trip to a well-preserved kauri-driving dam leads up the Kaiaraara Valley through kohekohe forest and nikau palm groves. The Kaiaraara dam (40 metres wide and 14 metres high) is one of the largest of some 3,000 dams built in New Zealand during the nineteenth and twentieth centuries to drive kauri logs downstream from inland areas to the coast to be rafted to mills.

Penne pasta with Italian sausage, fennel and tomato sauce

3 good-quality Italian pork sausages
1 red onion, chopped
1 tsp fennel seeds
4 tbsp olive oil
1 tsp dried rosemary
1 x 440 g can Italian tomatoes, chopped
250 g dried penne pasta
½ cup grated Grana Padana or good-quality Parmesan
salt and pepper to taste

Break or cut up the (raw) sausages into pieces 1–2 cm long. In the pan, sauté the onion and fennel seeds in the olive oil until soft. Add the rosemary and sausage pieces and sauté a further 3–4 minutes.

Add the tomatoes and bring to the boil. Reduce the heat and simmer for 10–15 minutes. Meanwhile, boil the pasta in plenty of salted water until cooked. Drain well and stir 2 tbsp of the cheese through it. Add the sausage sauce and pour into bowls. Top with the rest of the cheese.

Vegetarian option
Replace the sausage with 200 g red capsicum, sliced into 5 mm wedges.

If you only have one stove, cook the sausage mixture for 10 minutes, then take it off the heat and cook the pasta. When the pasta is done, return the sausage mixture to the stove and cook through for a further 4 minutes.

Vavasour Claudia's Vineyard Sauvignon Blanc (Awatere)

The fruit for this Awatere wine was harvested in the cool of night to retain flavour and freshness. Careful winemaking and specific yeast strains were employed so that the vibrant fruit flavours could be preserved. This wine shows lifted passionfruit and tropical notes. The palate exhibits the same fine fruit flavours with an underlying flinty note typical of Awatere Valley fruit. The finish is crisp and dry. We recommend the 2004 vintage, which is ready to drink now and over the next year or so.

Alternative wine
Clearview Unoaked Chardonnay (Hawke's Bay)

If you are feeling fit, climb Hirakimata. This involves a three-hour walk from Kaiaraara to the summit, so you will need plenty of time for the return trip. Take in the superb views from the highest point on the island (621 metres) and see the nesting burrows of the rare black petrel and some of the island's endemic plants such as *Olearia allomii* (a tree daisy) and *Kunzea sinclairii* (Great Barrier kanuka)

For the less energetic, Bushs Beach, about half an hour's walk west, is a great swimming spot.

There are also several pools in the Kaiaraara Stream that are worth exploring if the weather is hot and you're not too much of a wimp.

Great Barrier kanuka (*Kunzea sinclairii*).

Gillian Crowcroft

General tips
If you do make the effort to visit Great Barrier, we suggest spending more than just a couple of days on the island – there's plenty to see and do, even if it's just relaxing on the beautiful sandy beaches on the east coast.

Pinnacles Hut
Coromandel Forest Park

3 hours   80 bunks   Yes

Moderate

Year round

NZMS 260 T12 Thames

The Coromandel Forest Park was created in 1971 and covers 65,000 hectares of rimu, tawa and kauri forest. The highest point on the peninsula is Moehau (892 metres).

Time required
This tramp takes about three hours, plus a further two hours (round trip) if you want to climb up to the Pinnacles.

The best time to go
This tramp can be done year round, but school parties often use the hut in March.

Getting there
The nearest town to the start of the tramp is Thames, at the south of the Coromandel Peninsula. From there it is a 15-kilometre drive to the start of the tramp at the end of the road up the Kauaeranga River valley.

You will pass the DOC office several kilometres before the start of the track. We recommend you stop here to pick up your hut pass and check the weather reports. It pays not to leave any valuables in your vehicle, even though security is pretty good.

The shopping
Most of the ingredients, if not all, will be available in Thames.

The tramp
The Pinnacles Track follows the old packhorse trails from the carpark, over the river and up the valley. If you are fit it will only take two hours to the hut, but we recommend taking your time (three to four hours). The track used to be a supply route for millers and tree-fellers who cleared hundreds of acres of kauri from the valleys.

On the packhorse track to the Pinnacles Hut.

Rob Suisted

View from the summit of the
Pinnacles, looking east over the
Coromandel Peninsula.
Rob Suisted

The track was upgraded in the late 1990s and rebuilt in the form it had at the start of the century. The result is impressive – stone steps, wide enough for packhorses, dominate most of the track, which crosses the river three times as it rises steeply to the old logging camp. This was also used as a base for the power company to helicopter in the huge power lines that feed power from Thames to Tairua.

It takes 20–30 minutes from the car park to the first junction. From here the track undulates a little and rises steeply to the first swingbridge. If the water level is low you can walk across the rocks, but use your common sense. From this swingbridge the stone stairs come into play, and it's about an hour and a half from here to the logging camp. It is not all stairs, but they are what you will remember most. There are two more swingbridges, and from the last one it is about 20 minutes to the site of the logging camp. This is just a

Spiced salmon fillet with sweetcorn and couscous cakes

Sweetcorn and couscous cakes

½ cup couscous
½ cup boiling water
1 cup canned or frozen corn kernels
1 tsp ground cumin
pinch of crushed dried chillies
½ tsp salt
¼ tsp ground black pepper
1 spring onion, finely sliced
1 large egg, beaten
zest of half a lemon
canola oil for frying

Combine the couscous and the boiling water and set aside for 5–10 minutes. Add all the remaining ingredients to the couscous and mix well. Divide the mixture into four equal portions and press into round cakes about 2 cm high.

Heat the oil in a frying pan. (You really need a non-stick pan for this recipe.) Place the couscous cakes in the hot oil and cook until golden on the first side. When the bottom is crunchy, turn the cakes over carefully. Fry on the other side for a further 4–5 minutes until done. Don't worry if the cakes break up slightly – they'll still taste delicious. Set aside.

Salmon

2 x 180 g boneless salmon fillets (not skinless)
½ tsp ground coriander
½ tsp ground cumin
¼ tsp ground fennel seeds
¼ tsp salt
black pepper
200 g broccoli or green beans
2 lemon wedges

Make a few deep slashes on the skin side of the salmon. Combine the spices and the salt and pepper and sprinkle over both sides of the salmon fillets. Heat the oil in the pan until hot and place the salmon skin-side down. Lower the heat to medium and cook for 4 minutes. Turn the salmon over and cook for a further minute or until done to your liking. Leaving it a little on the rare side is good – it keeps the salmon juicy and moist.

Meanwhile, boil or steam the broccoli or beans.

Serve with a squeeze of lemon.

Vegetarian option

3 tomatoes, sliced
1 avocado, sliced
180 g mozzarella, cubed
basil leaves, torn

Dressing

2 tbsp olive oil
juice of half a lemon
1 clove garlic
salt and pepper

Combine the dressing ingredients, toss through the other ingredients and serve with the couscous cakes.

Stonecroft Gewürztraminer (Hawke's Bay)

We recommend the 2002 vintage, in which beautiful fruit has produced a well-balanced, weighty, textured wine. It has aromas of lychees and roses, which are followed by a full, almost creamy palate. A Turkish Delight character gives way to a weighty mid-palate and a fine lingering spice that goes on forever. This is a fine wine with great cellaring potential. More recent vintages are very similar, particularly the 2006.

Alternative wine

2003 Kaimara Estate Reisling (Nelson)

The Pinnacles.
Carl Nanning

Climbing a ladder on the track to
the Pinnacles.
Rob Suisted

clearing now and a good place for a rest and a moment to appreciate how high you've climbed.

There's a longdrop hidden in the trees at the northern end. From the logging camp it is an undulating walk of up to an hour to the Pinnacles Hut. The following day you could either go back down the stairs, or go down via the Billy Goat Trail.

The hut

This huge hut sleeps 80 people in two bunkrooms. It is a vast improvement on the previous one, which is now the warden's house. The hut even has showers (albeit cold), a gas kitchen and solar-powered lighting.

Things to do nearby

We recommend you leave your pack at the hut and climb for 45 minutes up to the Pinnacles. Although not a dangerous trip, it's not for the faint-hearted. There are some steep rock faces and several ladders to be negotiated before you arrive at a narrow ledge from which there are superb views of both sides of the Coromandel.

General tips

The Kauaeranga Valley has many short walks and several camping spots, so you might like to take a few extra days to explore the area properly. There are plenty of attractions in the region, such as the Driving Creek railway north of Thames. On the eastern side of the peninsula are numerous beautiful beaches, including Hahei and Hot Water Beach. The latter is famous for its warm springs, reached by digging into the sand at low tide.

The Tapu–Coroglen road is a lovely drive, with the added attraction of a square kauri that is 41 metres tall – signposted just west of the highest point of the road, involving a short walk of a few metres.

Sandy Bay Hut
Te Urewera National Park

Most trampers come to this area to do the Waikaremoana Great Walk, a three- to four-day lakeside tramp through beech and podocarp forest. This gourmet trip visits a smaller lake to the north. You need to book bunks in the hut at DOC's Aniwaniwa visitor centre.

Lake Waikaremoana ('sea of rippling waters') was formed 2,200 years ago when a huge landslide blocked a narrow gorge along the Waikaretaheke River. The lake is over 240 metres deep and covers 54 square kilometres. Te Urewera is home to the Tuhoe, the local Maori iwi. The story goes that Hine-pokohu-rangi came from the sky, luring Te Maunga (the mountain) to earth with her. Their child, Tuhoepotiki, a mortal being, is said to be the ancestor of the Tuhoe people.

2½ hours   18 bunks   No

Easy

Late January–February

NZMS 260 W18 Waikaremoana

Time required
This tramp will take about two and a half hours, unless you have a long break for lunch and swimming when you first arrive at the lake.

The best time to go
Te Urewera National Park is busy over Christmas so, if you want peace and quiet, avoid the December–January holiday period. In midwinter it can be very cold. February is the warmest month and one of the best times to go.

Getting there
The journey into Aniwaniwa, just beyond Waikaremoana in Te Urewera National Park, is one of the most exciting road trips in the country. You can approach it from Rotorua through Murupara (about 90 kilometres from Lake Waikaremoana) on State Highway 38. Alternatively, you can drive from Wairoa and the East Coast, again on State Highway 38. Either way, it is a great drive, climbing and winding and finally dropping

Sandy Bay Hut on the shore of Lake Wakareiti.

Dave King

down to the edge of the lake. Most of the road through the park is unsealed, so don't expect to rush. Slow down and enjoy the scenery.

The shopping

Don't rely on buying food when you arrive at Waikaremoana. We recommend you shop before you leave Rotorua or Wairoa, as only a minimal selection of food and drink is available within the national park. The local motor camp stocks some essentials but not the specialist foods required for this meal.

The tramp

This is one of the most beautiful tramps in the country. The journey up through beech forest to Lake Wakareiti (sister to Lake Waikaremoana) is simply magical. Riflemen and tomtits watch you on your journey through the largest expanse of native forest remaining in North Island. This track and hut now form part of the Waikaremoana Great Walk.

View from Sandy Bay Hut across Lake Wakareiti.
Dave King

From the Aniwaniwa visitor centre, cross the bridge and follow the signs directing you up into beech forest. You climb steadily up through the forest along a well-graded track for about an hour before emerging beside Lake Wakareiti, surrounded by native forest. There is a day shelter here, which apart from Sandy Bay Hut is the only building on the lake.

A further easy five-kilometre walk around the lake through beech forest and you will arrive at Sandy Bay Hut. There is no camping allowed within 500 metres of the track (including the lake edge) except within 50 metres of the hut. If you do the tramp in summer, look out for the tree fuchsia flowers that carpet the ground in December and January.

It is also possible to hire rowboats from the visitor centre for 24 hours. The trip is then reduced to a two-hour journey (one hour of walking up to Lake Wakareiti from the visitor centre and another hour's leisurely row, provided a strong nor'wester isn't blowing). If you do take a boat, stop off at Rahui Island on the way. This is one of four islands in the lake, and the only one you can land on. Because these islands have no possums, they carry the highest densities of *Peraxilla* and *Alepis* mistletoes in the North Island.

When you reach the hut, pull the boat up onto the shore so it doesn't float away in the night. A DOC fact sheet is available from the visitor centre, but it was written in 1997 and so is slightly out of date.

Fucshia excoticarta.
Jeremy Rolfe

The hut

Sandy Bay Hut, on the northeastern shore of Lake Wakareiti, is 'old style', but this adds to its charm. It is in good condition and the location is so special, no one cares about whether the accommodation is posh. The hut sleeps 18 in two bunk-rooms, with the kitchen/dining room between. It is just metres from the lake edge and surrounded by red and silver beech forest. There is gas heating at the hut.

Things to do nearby

No motorised craft are allowed on the lake, but DOC does rent out rowboats. This restriction means the lake retains its sense of peace and wilderness, and is particularly beautiful in the mornings as the sun rises out of the mist.

Cider chicken with blue cheese mash and broccoli

This meal takes a bit longer to cook than others in this book, but it is worth it – even for the aromas that fill the hut.

350 g chicken thighs
salt and pepper to taste
100 ml olive oil
1 large apple (Granny Smith is good), cored and sliced
4 cloves garlic
1 tsp dried rosemary (or 2 tsp fresh)
about 150 ml cider
1 head of broccoli or broccolini
500 g potatoes, peeled and cut into 3 cm chunks
100 g blue cheese
parsley, chopped

Season the chicken with salt and pepper. Heat a third of the oil in a frying pan and brown the chicken pieces on both sides. Remove from the pan.

Heat a further third of the oil in the pan and sauté the apple slices and 2 whole garlic cloves over a low heat until softened. Add the rosemary and the rest of the garlic, finely chopped. Transfer the chicken back to the pan and pour in the cider. Simmer for about 15 minutes until the chicken is cooked through.

Meanwhile, bring some water to the boil and blanch the broccoli or broccolini florets for 2 minutes. Scoop out of the pan and set aside. Put the potato chunks into the same water and cook until tender. Mash with the remaining olive oil and salt and pepper, then crumble the blue cheese into it and mix through.

Place the broccoli on top of the chicken mixture in the frying pan and let it reheat in the steam. Spoon the potato onto your plates, with the chicken and juices and broccoli on the side. Scatter with chopped parsley.

Wither Hills Chardonnay (Marlborough)

The aromas of this silky, elegant wine are the classic essence of cool-climate, late-ripened, small-cluster Marlborough chardonnay. Look for tropical fruit such as pineapple and melon, and wonderful stone-fruit characters on the palate. The flavours of Wither Hills Chardonnay will become more complex with time, and often you will be rewarded if you cellar the bottles for several years for a future gourmet tramp.

Alternative wines

Lawson's Dry Hill Pinot Gris (Marlborough)
Fairhall Downs Chardonnay (Marlborough)

This is a great time for trout fishing. We recommend booking a rowing boat from the DOC visitor centre before you arrive. This costs $45 for 24 hours. Staff will issue you with a key to one of the boats, which you will find tied up near the track when you arrive at the lake. Canoes and dinghies may also be hired from the motor camp.

The shores of Lake Wakareiti are one of the few places in New Zealand where you can lie in silence on a sandy lake-shore littered with tiny, multi-coloured beech leaves and listen to the native birdlife. In summer, a swim in the lake is a must before or after dinner.

Mountain beech foliage.
C. Rudge, DOC, Crown copyright

47

4 Whakapapaiti Hut

Tongariro National Park

2½ hours   20 bunks   No

Easy

Weekdays, March–May

NZMS 260 S20 Ohakune

Tongariro (left) and Ngauruhoe from the entrance to the park.
John Sawyer

Tongariro National Park was created in 1887 when land centring on the summits of the three volcanoes – Ruapehu, Ngauruhoe and Tongariro – was gifted to the nation by Te Heuheu, chief of Ngati Tuwharetoa. The original park was only 2,630 hectares but now covers approximately 80,000 hectares. At the time of its formation it was the first national park in New Zealand and only the fourth in the world.

While there is a risk of volcanic activity on Mt Ruapehu, there is a warning system in place to raise the alarm should a lahar sweep down the mountain. A lahar is a mix of water from a crater lake and the debris it picks up on its way

down the mountain. The most famous New Zealand lahar damaged a rail bridge at Tangiwai just before the Auckland–Wellington overnight train was due to cross it on Christmas Eve of 1953. Of the 285 people on board, 151 died. The last time Ruapehu erupted was in 1997.

Ranunculus nivicola, a mountain buttercup endemic to the North Island.
John Sawyer

Time required
This tramp will take two and a half hours if you start at Whakapapa Village, or less than an hour if you start at the Bruce Road car park. You will want a few hours of daylight to explore the area around the hut.

The best time to go
You can do this walk all year round, but in midwinter the ice and snow can make it a bit more of an adventure. Late summer or early spring is best, to see the alpine flowers at their peak, but avoid weekends at all costs.

Getting there
This tramp begins at, or near, Whakapapa Village in the Tongariro National Park, central North Island. This is accessible by road on State Highway 1 or by train to National Park. You can start either in Whakapapa village, as described here, or from the car park three kilometres up Bruce Road. Don't leave valuables in your car, as thieves are active in the park.

The shopping
If driving (or catching the train) from Wellington or Auckland, buy your provisions before you set off or do your shopping en route in Taupo or Taihape.

Ourisia vulcanica.
Heidi Meudt

The tramp
This tramp should not take longer than three hours at most. If it does, then you are either not very fit or you have missed the hut and are on your way to Ohakune.

From the visitor centre at Whakapapa, walk up the road about 200 metres. The track is signposted on the right-hand side of the road and starts in beech forest, crossing a large bridge perfect for playing Pooh sticks. The track goes around the mountain, climbing and then, annoyingly, descending

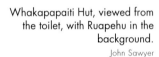
Whakapapaiti Hut, viewed from the toilet, with Ruapehu in the background.
John Sawyer

again, crossing small streams and open clearings from which you have fantastic views of Ngauruhoe and Ruapehu. If you see trees wrapped in silver or brown metal bands, look up into the branches for the mistletoes they are protecting from possum browse. In January the mistletoes will be more obvious than the bands, with their fabulous blaze of bright red flowers.

The track then starts to descend until you arrive at the Whakapapaiti River valley and cross a long-span wooden bridge. Shortly after this you arrive at a junction: the track to the hut is straight on up the valley. If you turn right here, you'll walk out of the park to Mangahuia campsite and the main highway.

The route is poled in case snow is covering the track. The track climbs gently, crosses the river again (this time without a bridge but with plenty of large rocks to hop across without getting wet), then climbs up through more beech forest until you arrive at the hut, about 45 minutes from the last junction.

The next morning you can return the same way, but we recommend a round trip, which takes about an hour and a half to the road and another hour (at least) back to Whakapapa. Set off east from the hut and climb steadily through patches of beech forest and shrubs, alongside the river, with views of waterfalls and Ruapehu directly ahead. This track climbs up onto a ridge of solidified lava that offers a vista of all three volcanoes.

The cone of Ngauruhoe can be admired from many tracks near Whakapapa.
John Sawyer

From the ridge, the track drops gently, then crosses relatively flat scoria covered by low scrub dominated by celmisias, dracophyllums and hebes. After about an hour (maybe more if you are unfit or tired) you reach the car park on Bruce Road. From here it is a gentle one-hour walk down to Whakapapa village.

The hut

The hut is a smart wooden building situated on the raised terrace of the Whakapapaiti River and nestled among patches of beech forest and open scrub of hebes and celery pine. There is no gas or cooking equipment at the hut, but a beautiful wood-burning stove sits in the middle. The hut sleeps 20. If you arrive early, we recommend you take the smaller dormitory to the left.

Olearia nummulariifolia.
John Sawyer

Things to do nearby

Leave the door open when you use the toilet and enoy a fantastic view of the hut and Ruapehu. Explore the Whakapapaiti valley either upstream or down – whichever way you go there is much to see. The plant life is extraordinary, especially in the summer months.

It is worth climbing up the valley to watch the amazing sunset, but remember to take a torch so you can return safely to the hut.

The woolly mountain daisy *Celmisia incana* can be seen along the track near Whakapapaiti Hut
John Sawyer

Pork fillet with lemon, olives and couscous

Couscous (from the Arabic word kouskous and the Berber word k'seksu) is a staple in North Africa and the national dish of Algeria, Morocco and Tunisia. It is also consumed in the Middle East, where it is called mughrabiyya. Couscous is the perfect tramping food, as it is light but filling and cooks in a flash.

350 g pork fillet (or lamb tenderloins, back-straps
   or stir-fry cut)
4 tbsp olive oil
1 medium onion, chopped
2 cloves garlic, chopped
1 tsp ground cumin
1 tsp ground coriander
1 lemon
½ cup green olives (stuffed is fine if that is all you can find)
1 tsp sugar or honey
2 tbsp tomato paste
150 g couscous
salt and pepper to taste
2 tbsp chopped coriander or parsley

Cut the pork fillet into 1 cm slices. Heat 2 tbsp of the olive oil in your frying pan and sear the meat quickly on both sides. Remove from the pan.

Heat the remaining oil and sauté the onion and garlic over a low heat until soft. Add the cumin and coriander. Thinly peel the rind off half the lemon and chop into very fine strips. Add to the pot and cook with spices for a minute or two.

Return the pork to the pan with the olives, sugar and tomato paste. Drizzle in some water if necessary to stop it sticking, and simmer gently for 10 minutes.

Meanwhile, cook the couscous by bringing to the boil ½ cup of water, with 1–2 tbsp of olive oil and 1 tsp of salt. Remove from the heat and pour in the couscous. Cover and stand for 2–3 minutes. Stir with a fork just before serving.

Season the meat well and serve over the couscous, garnished with the coriander or parsley. For a stronger lemon flavour, squeeze lemon juice over the top dish before serving.

Trinity Hill Chardonnay (Hawke's Bay)

The characters typical of Trinity Hill's Gimblett Road vineyards – mineral, grapefruit, fig and pear – are evident in this wine. Mealy, biscuity barrel ferment and integrated oak characters add complexity. The wine displays the desirable character of elegance with power. While this is a big wine, it also shows softness, finesse and balance.

Alternative wines

Lawson's Dry Hills Pinot Gris (Marlborough)
Fairhall Downs Chardonnay (Marlborough)

Bayview Chateau Tongariro, the only hotel in New Zealand in a World Heritage Area and a national park.
John Sawyer

General tips

The Bayview Chateau Tongariro is a splendid place to celebrate the completion of your tramp with a gin and tonic while lounging in a big comfy sofas facing the huge windows that overlook Tongariro and Ngauruhoe. This grandiose hotel was built in 1929 to provide an international standard of accommodation for overseas guests. In the main lounge there is a huge snooker table and a piano, so plenty of things to do. (Better to shower before you arrive or you may not quite blend in with the real guests.)

No trip to Tongariro National Park is complete without a soak in the private thermal pools at Tokaanu, 40 minutes' away at the southern end of Lake Taupo. If you have time, the short walk (less than two hours) around Lake Rotopounamu is one of New Zealand's most stunning. There have been reports of theft from vehicles in the car park, so don't leave anything valuable in your car (like the keys).

Maketawa Hut
Egmont National Park

Egmont National Park is dominated by the volcano that gave the park its name. There are two other volcanoes, Pouakai and Kaitake, but they are both dwarfed by Egmont (now also known as Taranaki). An area on the mountain was first protected in 1881, but it was not until 1900 that the national park was designated.

1½ hours   16 bunks   No

Easy

February–March

NZMS 260 P20 Egmont

Time required
This is an easy hour and a half tramp from the car park at the North Egmont visitor centre. You will need a lot more time (practically an entire day) if you plan to scale Taranaki.

Climbing through alpine scrub on the Taranaki summit track from Maketawa Hut.
John Sawyer

Maketawa Hut on the ridge line at left with Ruapehu just visible in the distance.
John Sawyer

On the lower route to Maketawa Hut.
John Sawyer

The best time to go
For the best weather and the fewest trampers we recommend late February and early March. If you want to see the native plants in flower, tramp in December or January.

Getting there
This tramp starts at the car park at the end of Egmont Road, where you can leave your car safely. The nearest main centre is New Plymouth, 30 minutes' drive along State Highway 3.

The shopping
We recommend you buy all your provisions in New Plymouth. If coming from the south via Stratford, you can buy your ingredients there.

The tramp
This tramp is part of the low-level track around the mountain to Dawson Falls. From the North Egmont car park, follow the signs for Summit Road for about 40 minutes until you arrive at the base of what is known as 'The Puffer', a steep grunt up to Tahurangi Lodge en route to the summit of Taranaki. Follow the signs at the bottom of 'The Puffer' to Maketawa Hut. The track follows the ridge back down the mountain through montane forest. You will be able to see the hut in the distance as you descend the ridge. Alternatively,

View from the deck of the hut towards New Plymouth.
John Sawyer

if the weather is bad when you arrive at the car park, take the lower track that is signposted to Maketawa. This takes an hour and a half through forest to the hut. The most striking feature of this walk is the horopito foliage that lines the track. Whichever route you take, come back the other way to make it a round trip.

The hut

Maketawa Hut was built in 1987 and has been recently up-graded. It is typical of many of the huts in the Egmont National Park. It is located on the Maketawa Track above Little Maketawa Stream on the northern slopes of Mt Taranaki. It is nestled among earthy-coloured leatherwoods, mountain totara, stunted kamahi, blechnum ferns, coprosma and five-finger where alpine scrub meets montane forest. From the hut deck there are commanding views of the Taranaki region and the upper slopes of the mountain.

Horopito (*Pseudowintera colorata*) foliage.
John Sawyer

At night the lights from the region's towns form a ring below you on the plain: a stunning sight.

Maketawa Hut has two bunkrooms that each sleep eight, and is the only hut in the Egmont National Park with gas heating. The hut is serviced and has hand-washing facilities, mattresses and water on site. Half the hut is taken up by the kitchen and dining area.

Udon noodles with five-spice pork, mushrooms and bok choy

Japanese udon noodles, thought to have originated around 1450, are made from a mixture of wheat flour, water and salt that has been kneaded, ripened, rolled flat and cut into strips. The noodles are then boiled and served in hot broth or with a dipping sauce.

We recommend you take a small grater to mince the ginger and grate the garlic.

½ tsp five-spice powder
½ tsp ground ginger
2 tsp brown sugar
2 cloves garlic, grated or chopped
½ tsp salt
½ tsp black pepper
1 pork fillet (about 300–320 g), sinew removed
3 tbsp vegetable oil
1 tbsp minced ginger
2 tbsp soy sauce
120 g brown button, oyster (phoenix) or needle
    mushrooms, sliced
750 ml vegetable or chicken stock (or use 2 stock cubes)
3 baby bok choy, sliced in half lengthways

400 g udon noodles (2 x 200 g packets)
salt and pepper
2 spring onions, sliced thinly on the diagonal

Combine the five-spice, powdered ginger, 1 tsp brown sugar, garlic, salt and pepper and coat the pork fillet with this. Heat 1 tbsp of the oil in a frying pan and sear the pork fillet for 3–4 minutes. Set aside.

In a pot, sauté the minced ginger in the rest of the oil, add the second tsp of brown sugar, the soy sauce and mushrooms and cook a further minute. Add the stock and bring to the boil. Reduce to a simmer and cook for 10 minutes. Add the bok choy and noodles and simmer for a further 2–3 minutes. Season to taste, and add the sliced spring onion.

Divide the noodles and broth between two bowls. Chop the pork into 5 mm slices on the diagonal. Add the pork to the bowls and leave to stand for 3–5 minutes before eating. The residual heat in the broth will cook the pork a little more, so it is succulent and tender.

Vegetarian option
Replace the pork with 400 g zucchini, sliced diagonally. Coat the zucchini with the five-spice mix as above, and fry lightly for 2 minutes. Replace the chicken stock with vegetable stock, and double the quantity of mushrooms to 240 g.

Odyssey Reserve Iliad Chardonnay (Gisborne)

This is an elegant, concentrated wine, full and vibrant, often with rich peach and melon as well as fig and grapefruit flavours and well-integrated nutty French oak. It is beautifully balanced and a perfect match for this meal.

Alternative wine
2003 Felton Road Dry Riesling (Central Otago)

Blechnum novaezelandiae.
John Sawyer

Things to do nearby

If you have lots of energy to spare and it's early in the day when you arrive, leave your pack at the hut and head for the summit of Taranaki (2,518 metres). You will need plenty of food, water and waterproofs with you, as conditions can change at a moment's notice. The round trip takes about seven hours. Walk back to the start of 'The Puffer' and tackle the slope to the private Tahurangi Lodge. Then climb up the staircase and follow the poles along the ridge to the summit.

An evening drink and star-gazing back on the deck of the hut will round out a fabulous day.

General tips

If you can afford the time, it is worth taking a surfboard (in your car, not your pack) and heading down the Taranaki coast on State Highway 45 – the 'Surf Highway' – to Oakura, Okato and Opunake. These are great spots to relax for a few days after the tramp. Taranaki is a beautiful part of the country – a lost world.

Ti toi, mountain cabbage trees
(*Cordyline indivisa*).
John Sawyer

Powell Hut

Tararua Forest Park

The Tararua Forest Park stretches from the Manawatu Gorge to the Rimutaka Saddle, and was established in 1954 by the Forest Service. The highest peaks are Mt Mitre (1,571 metres) and Mt Hector (1,529 metres), but Mt Holdsworth is a better introduction to the range. The Tararua Tramping Club was established in 1919, the country's first.

3½ hours   32 bunks   Yes

Moderate

Weekdays, year round

NZMS 260 S26 Carterton

Time required
This tramp will take just over three and a half hours, with an additional hour and a half return to the summit of Holdsworth.

The best time to go
This tramp can be done year round, though from October to mid-December it can be a bit wet and windy. The track is used more often at the weekend, so if you want space to cook at the hut we recommend a weekday trip. The red-flowered mistletoe (*Peraxilla tetrapetala*), generally rare in the Tararua Forest Park, can be seen in full flower in December at the start of the tramp. The alpine plants are in full bloom from December to February.

Fewer people do the full Mt Holdsworth circuit between May and October, so this time might be best if you want the hut to yourself. Be warned that the Tararua Ranges receive six metres of rain each year, and some of this will fall on you.

Getting there
To get to the start of this tramp you must first journey to the Wairarapa. The nearest town is Masterton, at the north of the Wairarapa Plains on State Highway 2. It is 90 minutes' drive from Wellington and an hour from Palmerston North. There are regular buses and trains from Wellington. The problem you face, if you do not have a car, is getting from

DOC sign on the track from Powell Hut to the summit of Holdsworth.
John Sawyer

Tararua matipo (*Myrsine umbricola*) is endemic to this area and was only recognised as a new species in 2003.

John Sawyer

Masterton to the start of the tramp at Holdsworth Lodge. You could try hitching, but with all that food and wine you might be mugged. Better to take a taxi and arrange with the driver to pick you up the next day at a predetermined time, although it will cost up to $50 each way.

The shopping

You're bound to find some tasty pickles at Taste Delicious and the Main Street Deli (both in Greytown) to add to your picnic. You must stop at The French Baker (one of New Zealand's finest), also in Greytown, on the morning of your tramp to buy at least one loaf for your meal (you may want two – with the other for before dinner or for lunch en route).

If you are coming from Wellington, there are roadside stalls to buy your vegetables, and butchers in Greytown and Carterton for the steak. You may want to buy the eggplant before you set off, as they are not always be available in local shops.

If you don't fancy our wine selection, alternatives can be purchased at one of the vineyards in southern Wairarapa or Martinborough (a slight detour but well worth it). Otherwise, Carrington and Deans is a great wine shop in Greytown. If arriving from the north, your choices are more limited – probably best to stock up in Palmerston North.

Hebe evenosa, another endemic plant of the Tararua Range, grows beside the hut.

John Sawyer

The tramp

This is a straightforward tramp, starting from the car park at Holdsworth Lodge. Remember to sign the intentions book here before you set off. The track is pretty much level at the start and well defined. It would have been a more difficult route in the past, before bridges were installed over Holdsworth Creek. You start by crossing a huge wooden bridge from which you can see epiphytic native *Earina* orchids growing on branches of beech trees that arch over the creek.

At the first junction, turn left up the Gentle Annie Track. This climbs steadily but is well graded. After just over an hour you will arrive at Pig Flat, where the track levels off and drops down to a small newly built shelter. Ignore the turn-off on your left, which will take you down to Totara Flats and the Waiohine Gorge.

The track then climbs steeply and, after an hour, runs along a ridge where you are surrounded by silver beech forest dripping with green lichens. The track continues through the treeline to emerge on an exposed rocky ridge. The last section is a bit of a scramble, but after half an hour you will arrive at the hut.

Powell Hut, perched on the slopes of Mt Holdsworth.
John Sawyer

Leatherwood (*Olearia colensoi* var. *colensoi*) is a common plant at the treeline on Mt Holdsworth.
John Sawyer

Ribeye steaks with caponata and crusty bread

Caponata is a Sicilian dish (but believed to be of Spanish origin), made from eggplant and other vegetables, often including pinenuts and anchovies. It is cooked in olive oil and served at room temperature, often as an antipasto relish. Here we team it with steak and crusty bread as a hearty main meal. This meal can be eaten a couple of days into a longer tramp, as the steak will keep well in a cool part of your pack. If you can't find an eggplant, replace it with two more zucchini.

1 onion, finely chopped
2 cloves garlic, finely chopped
1 small eggplant (about 10 cm long), diced into 1.5 cm pieces
olive oil for frying
5 button mushrooms, sliced
½ red capsicum, diced into 1 cm pieces
1 tsp oregano
100 g tomato paste
1 tbsp capers
1 tsp sugar
1 small zucchini, diced into 1 cm pieces
4 tbsp stuffed green olives
2 x 200 g ribeye steaks/Scotch fillet
crusty bread

Sauté the onion, garlic and eggplant for 2 minutes in olive oil. Add the mushrooms and capsicum and cook a further 2 minutes. Pile in everything else except the olives (and steak!), adding water as necessary to stop it burning. Cook gently for about 20 minutes, adding the olives just before the end of cooking to heat through.

Get your frying pan very hot and cook the steak to your liking. Serve with caponata on the side and loads of crusty bread.

Vegetarian option
Unless you are a special sort of vegetarian you will have to leave out the steak. Shame. The caponata with crusty bread is a delicious meal in itself, but you may want to increase the quantities slightly.

The hut
Powell Hut, on the upper slopes of Mt Holdsworth, is large and new (the old one mysteriously burnt down in 1998). It sleeps 32 and is situated at the treeline. From it there are extensive views over the Wairarapa Plains and Lake Wairarapa to the south. The surrounding vegetation is interesting and unique, being composed of species endemic to this area (i.e. not found anywhere else in the world). *Hebe evenosa*, for example, forms large bushes in front of the hut.

Things to do nearby
The climb from the hut to the summit of Mt Holdsworth (1,570 metres) is beautiful. It takes about 40 minutes without a pack. You follow the ridge as it curves around to the north, climbing all the time through tussock grass and small

Matua Valley Matheson Syrah
This wine is produced from the syrah grape, more commonly known in Australia as shiraz. This is a well-focused syrah with a silky palate and finely meshed tannins. It has a youthful style that exhibits nuances of herb, blackberry and plum, together with a hint of pepper. Whatever the vintage, you cannot beat this wine to accompany this gourmet meal.

Alternative wines
Sacred Hill Broken Stone Merlot (Hawke's Bay)
Crab Farm Merlot (Hawke's Bay)

On the track to the summit of
Mt Holdsworth.

John Sawyer

gardens of alpine plants. One reason for making the climb is to watch the sunset or sunrise. The views to the west of ridge after ridge of uplifted greywacke are amazing. Turn around and you see the Wairarapa Plains and, in the distance, the rugged eastern Wairarapa taipos (hills) and the Aorangi Range.

General tips

There are plenty of wineries, op shops and café/delis in the Wairarapa, all of which are worth spending time exploring. Martinborough is a major wine centre, where you can try many of the region's fabulous labels. North of Masterton is DOC's Mt Bruce National Wildlife Centre, which houses some of New Zealand's rarest birds, such as kaka and takahe.

Mt Arthur Hut
Kahurangi National Park

7

Mt Arthur provides a superb introduction to Kahurangi, one of the country's newest and most diverse national parks. It was established in 1996, but the area is known to have been occupied from the fourteenth century by Maori. This is truly a *Lord of the Rings*-esque place and a perfect destination for a spot of gourmet tramping.

1¼ hours   8 bunks   Yes

Easy

Weekdays, year round

NZMS 260 M27 Mt Arthur

Time required

This tramp takes just over an hour and a quarter from the car park, but we recommend that you allow a full day so you can climb Mt Arthur before returning to the hut for a well-earned meal.

Looking from the summit of Mt Arthur across the tablelands to Salisbury Lodge and Balloon Hut.
John Sawyer

The best time to go

The best time to head through the Upper Moutere, to the start of this tramp, is when the new local-vintage sauvignon blanc has just been released (late September/early October). We recommend you avoid weekends, as you will find half of Nelson in the hut with you on a Friday or Saturday night, or at least clogging up the track doing day walks.

Getting there

The nearest major town is Nelson, and the easiest way to get there is to fly, although the road trip (from anywhere) is beautiful. Whether you drive from Christchurch (through the Lewis Pass), from Picton and Blenheim (along the Queen Charlotte Drive), or from the West Coast (through Murchison) you will appreciate why so many people are choosing to live in Nelson. The start of this tramp is the Flora car park at the head of the Graham Valley on the west bank of the Motueka River. Regular track transport is available from Nelson.

The shopping

Nelson is the place to buy your food, except for the smoked salmon, which you must buy in Mapua at The Smokehouse. There is a bewildering range of manuka-smoked products on sale here – salmon, other fish and meats, paté and sauces.

The Dr Seuss tree or mountain neinei
(*Dracophyllum traversii*).
John Sawyer

Mt Arthur Hut.
John Sawyer

Don't stop at the café for too long or you'll be tempted to scrap the tramp altogether.

Stop at a local vineyard in the Upper Moutere Valley for the wine. Some of the best are Kahurangi, Seifried and Neudorf, although for this meal we recommend the excellent Alexia riesling. A wide range of speciality shops in the area, including Tasman Bay Olives, can provide your ingredients.

The tramp

This straightforward easy-grade tramp is one of the shortest in the book. It begins with a wide gravel path, originally a miners' track, which takes you quickly to the Flora Saddle. From here you take the left-hand fork for the three-kilometre gentle climb to the Mt Arthur Hut at the bush edge.

One of the most striking parts of the trip is the walk through a forest of mountain neinei (*Dracophyllum traversii*). These trees look like huge pineapple plants or something straight out of a Dr Seuss book. Their deep red flowerheads are spectacular alongside the silver and mountain beech trees covered in lichen, and the rough-leaved tree daisy (*Olearia lacunosa*). Through the trees you will enjoy tantalising glimpses of the valleys below.

Climbing to the summit of Mt Arthur.
John Sawyer

Hot-smoked salmon Niçoise salad

'Niçoise' means the dish originated in Nice, in southern France. The Niçoise salad is probably the most famous of these.

Vacuum-packed salmon lasts well, so this meal can be eaten up to three days into a tramp if you want.

250 g washed baby potatoes (Desirée are good,
      or new-season)
200 g long green beans
1 clove garlic
50 ml extra-virgin olive oil
5 medium tomatoes (preferably vine-ripened)
2 hard-boiled free-range eggs
300–350 g fillet hot-smoked salmon
small can of anchovies
100 g crespelli or Niçoise black olives
salt and pepper to taste

Put the potatoes into a pot of boiling salted water. Cook for 12 minutes, then add the beans to the pot and boil for a further 4 minutes. Meanwhile, crush the garlic with some salt and stir it into the olive oil.

Toss the potatoes and beans in half the olive oil and garlic mixture, then place on a serving plate. Halve the

Vegetarian option
Leave out the salmon and anchovies and add 50 g of caperberries.

tomatoes and eggs and place these around the vegetables. Place the salmon fillet on top and drape a lavish number of anchovies around the plate. Scatter with olives. Season to taste and drizzle the remaining oil and garlic mixture over the top before serving.

If you would like a warm meal, heat the salmon through in a frying pan for a minute or two each side.

Alexia Sauvignon Blanc (Nelson)

On the nose this sauvignon blanc often exhibits strong lime and ripe capsicum aromas with some aromatic curranty and gooseberry characters. A broad spectrum of flavours, ranging from ripe capsicum through gooseberry and slightly minerally notes to the riper passionfruit, is evident on the palate.

Alternative wines
Astrolabe Sauvignon Blanc (Marlborough)
Felton Road Chardonnay (Central Otago)

The lancewood tree daisy (*Olearia lacunosa*) grows alongside the track to the hut.
John Sawyer

The hut

The Mt Arthur Hut sits just below the treeline above some marble sinkholes, which are depressions in the ground formed when acidic groundwater dissolves the underlying rock. LPG stoves are supplied for cooking. It is not a big hut, so arrive early if you want a bunk. There is some space for tents near the hut but even that can be full on a busy night.

Things to do nearby

Hike up onto the ridge and follow the poled route to the summit of Mt Arthur (1,795 metres). This will take a couple of hours from the hut. It is worth the climb for the 360-degree views of the Tasman Sea, Nelson and surrounding mountain ranges. To the south and west there are spectacular views of the Mt Owen Massif and the Kahurangi National Park. Take plenty of water, as none is available on the ridge. This route is exposed and can be treacherously windy in bad weather. In winter the ridge is usually covered in snow.

Even if you do not make the summit, it is interesting to spend some time above the treeline among the alpine plants, including speargrass, hebes, gentians, daisies and yellow buttercups.

On the Mt Arthur summit ridge.
John Sawyer

Another option is to continue for a second day (about five hours' walking) to Salisbury Lodge. This involves climbing the ridge towards Mt Arthur and, after about an hour, descending to the right down a steep track into a valley. You then traverse a series of hills, the tallest of which is Gordons Pyramid, from where you can see the hut on the Mt Arthur Tablelands, which stretch away to the west. The third day involves a hike out back to the car park through this easy country.

Looking down from Mt Arthur towards Nelson.
John Sawyer

General tips

You must visit at least one of the local wineries in the Upper Moutere Valley either on the way there or the way back. Lunch at the Mapua Smokehouse is highly recommended for fish and chips beside the estuary in the company of Hamish, a friendly kotuku (white heron) that visits the café from the end of March to October.

Heaphy Hut
Kahurangi National Park

4 hours   30 bunks   Yes
Moderate
Late February–March
NZMS 260 L26 Heaphy

The Heaphy River was named after Charles Heaphy, who, with Thomas Brunner (draughtsman and surveyor with the New Zealand Company) and Kehu, a Maori guide, was the first European to traverse the West Coast route. The river's original name is Whakapoai, named by the people who occupied the area from the sixteenth century. Many generations of Maori followed a trail over the Gouland Downs from the Aorere River to the Heaphy in search of pounamu (greenstone) for tools, weapons and ornaments. As with so many places in New Zealand, the European name has taken precedence over the original name.

Time required
This tramp will take a good four hours – more if you are not fit or spend time on the beaches during the walk in.

The best time to go
You need to book with DOC to do this tramp during the peak summer season. It can be done year round, although it gets busy during the last week in December and first two weeks of January. However, there are many reasons for doing the tramp at this time of year, not the least of them being the spectacle of southern rata (*Metrosideros umbellata*) in flower, forming a deep red cloak across the forest canopy.

Towards the end of summer you'll meet large numbers of children on their annual school camp. Late February to early March is probably the best time to go if you want a peaceful gourmet dinner meal. Why not combine this trip with a visit to the Wild Food Festival in Hokitika in March?

Southern rata (*Metrosideros umbellata*).
Greg Lind, DOC, Crown copyright

Getting there
The tramp starts 15 kilometres north of Karamea on the West Coast of the South Island. Most people arrive in

One of the many beaches on the
coastal section of the Heaphy Track.
Rob Suisted

Karamea by road (bus or car) from the larger coastal town
of Westport to the south, or across the Main Divide from
Christchurch. You can fly from Nelson to Karamea if you
want to get a different perspective of Kahurangi National
Park. Shuttle buses run to the shelter at the mouth of
the Kohaihai River and the start of the tramp.

The shopping
Shop before you leave home, or stock up in Westport if
you drive through.

The tramp
This tramp is the final segment of the Heaphy Track, one
of DOC's Great Walks. It was once an historic crossing from
Golden Bay to the West Coast for prospectors who rushed
for Karamea when gold was discovered there in 1861. You
may choose to walk the entire 82 kilometres, but gourmet
trampers will probably prefer to confine themselves to this

Spicy lamb meatballs with bulgar wheat, hummus and stir-fried zucchini and capsicum

Bulgar wheat (also known as burghul in the Middle East and North Africa) has a nutty flavour and is made from several species of wheat (usually durum). Its traditional production involves parboiling the grain and then drying by spreading it in the sun. The grain is then de-branned. It is the main ingredient in tabouleh, the classic Lebanese salad.

2 cups water
200 g bulgar wheat (often sold as cracked or kibbled wheat)
1 small onion, finely chopped
1 tsp each ground cumin and dried mint
½ tsp each dried chilli and cinnamon
salt and pepper to taste
350 g minced lamb
olive oil for frying
2 red capsicums, cut into quarters and deseeded
3 zucchini, sliced diagonally
1 x 200 g tub of hummus (we recommend Lisa's)

Bring the water to the boil and pour it into a bowl to just cover the bulgar wheat. Set aside.

Add the onion, spices and salt and pepper to the minced

Vegetarian option
This meal is delicious with falafels instead of meatballs. Take a plastic tub of falafel mix (Delicious Lebanese Snack or Olive Grove). Roll as much of the mixture as you need into small balls and brown these for 2–3 minutes. Alternatively, you can buy ready-made falafels that just need to be warmed through.

lamb and shape into balls. Heat some oil in the frying pan and brown the meatballs. Turn the heat down and cook for about 8 minutes until cooked through. Remove and keep warm. (If you have a lid, put it upside down on the frying pan during the next phase of cooking and place the meatballs in this.

Add some more oil to the pan and sauté the vegetables for 3–5 minutes, or to your liking. Thin the hummus with a little water. Spoon the bulgar wheat onto your plates, place the meatballs on it and spoon the hummus sauce over the top. Add the vegetables at the side.

section. It takes you through some of New Zealand's most fantastic coastal scenery, with nikau palm tree groves and beautiful beaches along the edge of the Tasman Sea.

Once you have crossed the long suspension bridge over the Kohaihai River you then climb a small saddle before dropping to Scotts Camp and a grassy clearing. Next you cross Swan Burn and continue on to Crayfish Point. The sign-posted track follows the bush edge for most of the journey, though at times you'll be drawn down to the beach so that you can take off your boots and walk barefoot on the sand. The approach to the Heaphy River takes you through

Akarua Pinot Noir (Central Otago)

Akarua Winery was established at Bannockburn, the world's southernmost winemaking region, in 1996 by Sir Clifford Skeggs. The landscape is mountainous, rising to over 2,000 metres, and the Akarua vines are planted among spectac-ular alpine scenery. This pinot – the vineyard's flagship wine – has complex aromas that range from fruits of the forest, cherries and thyme to smoked bacon and truffles, intermingled with hints of vanilla. The palate has classical elegance and finesse, with rich, velvety tannins that complement the vibrancy of the fruit and the silky texture.

Alternative wine
Mills Reef Elspeth Syrah (Hawke's Bay)
Babich Irongate Chardonnay (Hawke's Bay)

Oparara land snail (*Powelliphanta annectens*), one of New Zealand's endemic species of giant carnivorous land snail. Watch out for these near Heaphy Hut.
Ingrid Gruner

A grove of nikau palms (*Rhopalostylis sapida*) on the Heaphy Track.
Sonia Frimmel, DOC, Crown copyright

groves of nikau and karaka trees. The forest is lush with a simultaneous subtropical and subantarctic feel to it, and the roaring sea is a constant reminder that you are on the West Coast.

The mouth of the Heaphy is an exciting place, where the river surges out through a narrow passage to the sea. As waves wash in, the salt water and fresh water collide in spectacular fashion.

Native wildlife you could encounter on the tramp include weka, tui, bellbirds, woodpigeons (kereru) and robins. You may hear greater spotted kiwi at night, but it's unlikely you will see them. Native long-tailed bats (one of New Zealand's very few land mammals) emerge in the forest at dusk to feed on insects.

An extraordinary feature of the local fauna is the carnivorous land snail (*Powelliphanta*), forty species of which occur in this area. These shelter during the day and come out at night to feed on worms. They are fully protected by law, and even taking their empty shells is not permitted.

Swingbridge over Wekakura Creek, on the way to Heaphy Hut.
Rob Suisted

The hut

The hut is in a beautiful location above the Heaphy River and set back a couple of hundred metres from the coast. There are actually two buildings, but the old six-bed hut is now staff quarters. The newer one has 20 bunks and excellent views over the lagoon, Heaphy Bluff and the Tasman Sea.

Things to do nearby

Enjoy a swim in the lagoon at the mouth of the Heaphy River (not in the sea – the undertow will take you to Australia). Play cricket on the huge grassy campsite below the hut. At low tide you can cross the river and head north, climbing through a hole in Heaphy Bluff.

General tips

You'll need to buy a Heaphy Track hut and camp pass before doing this gourmet tramp. However, these do not guarantee a bunk in the hut, so if you want to be assured of a place then set out early and during a time of year when few people are on the track. The passes can be obtained at outdoor shops, hostels, transport companies, information centres and DOC offices. Note there is a two-night limit on staying at the Heaphy Hut.

There are plenty of short walks and places to see between Karamea and Westport. The Cow Shed Café is well worth a visit – it's world famous on the West Coast.

Nydia Hut
Marlborough Sounds

3 hours   50 bunks   Yes

Moderate

Year round

NZMS 260 P27 Picton

Nydia Bay was once the site of a Maori pa and its original name, Opouri, means 'place of sadness'. Legend has it that, before migrating to the Marlborough Sounds, the leader of a hapu (subtribe) sacrificed a young boy as an offering to Tangaroa (God of the Sea). When the boy's father found out, he and the rest of the tribe found the leader and killed him.

Please take care not to annoy anyone while you are there.

Time required

This tramp to the hut takes three hours from the water-taxi drop-off point at Shag Point, across from Havelock. The second day is a further three- to four-hour walk over to

Tennyson Inlet.
© Marco Nef, www.shima.ch

Tennyson Inlet. As this is a one-way tramp, you'll need to arrange to be picked up at the end.

The best time to go
This gourmet tramp can be done all year round, although school trips can make it busier in early February.

Getting there
The Nydia Track can be done in either direction. Here it is described from south to north (Havelock to Tennyson Inlet).

The nearest town is Havelock, on Queen Charlotte Drive from Picton to Nelson at the confluence of the Pelorus and Kaiuma Rivers. The only road access to Pelorus Sound is through Havelock.

If you choose to tramp from the Tennyson Inlet end, access is by road from Pelorus or Nelson, up the Rai Valley.

You can drive to the start of the tramp, at the end of Kaiuma Bay Road (32 kilometres north of Havelock), but it is much easier to take the five-minute water-taxi trip from Havelock to Shag Point. Although this adds a further three kilometres to the tramp, as you then have to walk to the Kaiuma car park, it saves the drive.

The shopping
Havelock is fine for last-minute provisions, but Nelson is the place to buy your food. If you are coming from Wellington, shop before you leave and buy the Cloudy Bay Sauvignon Blanc at the winery on your way through Marlborough.

The tramp
From Shag Point the tramp takes you over the Kaiuma Saddle (387 metres) and down to Nydia Bay. It then climbs up over the Nydia Saddle, before finally descending to Duncan Bay and Tennyson Inlet.

The track for the most part is well graded and signposted. The first section is nothing spectacular, although crossing the Kaiuma River can be exciting after heavy rain. The track rises through beech forest above the bay, before descending to Omanakie Stream. You then pass into forest again and climb until you reach the saddle. That's the hardest part

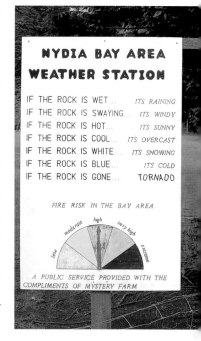

Sign at Nydia Bay.
© Marco Nef, www.shima.ch

Bush on the Nydia Track.
© Marco Nef, www.shima.ch

Chorizo and fennel risotto

Risotto is a classic rice dish of northern Italy, where it is often served as the first course of a larger meal. The addition of seafood, chicken or vegetables makes risotto suitable as a main course. Our version features sausage and fennel. If you can't obtain fennel bulbs, use your imagination to find a substitute. This meal can be eaten three to four days into a longer tramp.

Vegetarian option

Substitute 100 g asparagus and 100 g yams (or carrots) for the chorizo, and replace the chicken stock with vegetable stock. Before cooking the risotto, chop the yams into 5 mm pieces and boil for 6 minutes. Add the chopped asparagus to the same pot and boil for a further 2 minutes. Remove from the heat, drain and put to one side. Add these ingredients 5 minutes before the rice is fully cooked.

40 g butter
1 medium onion, finely chopped
2 cloves garlic, chopped
1 medium-sized fennel bulb, finely sliced
3 chorizo sausages, sliced on the diagonal
1 cup (220 g) Arborio rice
½ cup white wine
500 ml chicken stock (or use a stock cube)
salt and pepper to taste
¼–½ cup grated parmesan

Salad

2 tomatoes, chopped
mesclun lettuce
1 avocado, chopped
20 g pinenuts, lightly toasted

Heat the butter in a large pot and cook the onion, garlic and fennel over a gentle heat until soft. Add the sausage and the rice and cook, stirring frequently, for 2–3 minutes or until the rice becomes translucent.

Add the wine and keep stirring over the heat until all the liquid has been absorbed. Pour in the first cup of stock and turn down the heat. Stir continuously until all this liquid has been absorbed. Keep adding the rest of the stock and stirring occasionally until the rice is cooked but still firm to the bite. This can take up to half an hour. Season and stir in the grated parmesan.

Serve immediately with a tomato or crisp green salad.

over with. You can then relax and enjoy the descent into Nydia Bay along a gentle track that quickly emerges from beech forest to give good views of the bay and surrounding forest. The DOC hut is signposted to the right (30 minutes' walk) once you reach Nydia Bay.

The second day's walk takes you from the hut around the bay to the campsite. From the northern side of the campsite the track enters the bush and climbs steadily to the Nydia Saddle (347 metres), from where you can admire the sight of Tennyson Inlet. You then drop to Ngawhakawhiti Bay through

Cloudy Bay Sauvignon Blanc (Marlborough)

Cloudy Bay Sauvignon Blanc is famously pale straw green in colour and mouth-wateringly fragrant. It is redolent of a midsummer kitchen with aromas of ripe passionfruit, yellow plums, juicy limes and freshly picked basil. The palate is pure and refreshing, with concentrated flavours that echo the aromas, impeccably balanced acidity and a long, crisp finish. It's a fabulous wine that will perfectly accompany this gourmet meal.

Alternative wines
Matua Matheson Sauvignon Blanc (Hawke's Bay)
Margrain Pinot Noir (Martinborough)
The Escarpment Pinot Gris (Martinborough)

Nydia Bay from Nydia Saddle.
© Marco Nef, www.shima.ch

thick bush made up of beech, kamahi and punga (tree ferns).

If you're quiet you may meet fantails and other native birds along the way. At the coast the forest changes and the still-dominant beech becomes mixed with nikau palms and native conifers – rimu, matai and miro. From Ngawhakawhiti Bay the track follows a beautiful coastal route around to Duncan Bay. This is flat terrain, and if it is hot you may be tempted to swim.

The hut

Nydia Lodge is a huge hut – in fact it is a series of three bunkhouses with a kitchen and toilet facilities. Each bunk-house has three rooms with between three and seven bunks. It was built mainly for schools (the facility sleeps 50), but otherwise the hut is not heavily used. This makes it perfect for a gourmet tramp. There is a campsite at the northwest corner of the bay, but it will be harder to prepare your meal if you stay there and the additional walking time will seriously eat into Happy Hour.

Things to do nearby

Nydia Bay is a great place to relax or go for a swim in the sheltered waters. Without expending too much energy you can explore the coastline and the fringing beech forest.

General tips

Havelock is the self-proclaimed 'Green-lipped Mussel Capital of the World'. Sample the local fare at Musselboys, either before you leave or when you get back. If you are travelling back through to Blenheim, a visit to one of the multitude of Marlborough wineries is a must.

Angelus Hut
Nelson Lakes National Park

Nelson Lakes National Park marks the northern limit of the Southern Alps. The mountains here are dramatic and the wildlife is diverse. According to Maori mythology, the lakes in this park were created by Rakaihaitu using his ko (digging stick). Scientists say that glaciers did the job. Whatever you believe about the origins of Lake Rotoiti, it is a splendid place from which to embark upon a gourmet tramp.

Time required

This tramp is for fitter gourmets. You will need four hours to reach the hut from the water-taxi drop-off point, and a few more hours if you want to explore the alpine vegetation around Lake Angelus.

4 hours	36 bunks	No
	Hard	
	December–February	
	NZMS 260 M29 Murchison,	
	N29 St Arnaud, M30 Matakitaki	

View from the Robert Ridge into the cloud-filled Angelus Basin.
Rob Suisted

The best time to go

The ideal time to do this tramp is when there are no wasps (a serious prblem in this park) and when it is not raining. That cuts down your window of opportunity to perhaps one day in every 200. But that day is worth waiting for, since this tramp is one of the most beautiful in the country. We recommend December–February, because the alpine flowers will be in full bloom and the weather is more likely to be settled.

Getting there

Take a bus to St Arnaud from Nelson, or drive from West-port (up State Highway 6), or up the Wairau Valley from Blenheim or Picton. St Arnaud, gateway to the Nelson Lakes National Park, is a small village on State Highway 63.

The shopping

Food should be bought in Nelson (or Blenheim at a push). Pick up some wine from one of the vineyards in Nelson or the Wairau Valley, although for this meal we highly recommend the wonderful Pegasus Bay Riesling, which can be bought from the winery in Waipara, an hour's drive north of Christchurch, or from a good bottlestore. If you fly from Wellington to Picton, buy your food in the capital before you leave. Orchards up the Wairau Valley sell seasonal fruit, such as cherries in December.

The tramp

The tramp starts with a water-taxi trip from Kerr Bay to the head of Lake Rotoiti. You can walk the nine kilometres (three hours), but we recommend gourmet trampers enjoy the boat ride to the jetty near Coldwater Hut.

The signposted tramp from there takes you alongside Coldwater Stream in the wide Travers River valley. The track follows the Travers River for about two kilometres, then makes a hard right to climb steeply up the Cascade Track to Angelus Hut along the Hukere Stream. If you miss the turn-off for the Cascade Track then you will carry on for hours up the Travers River to John Tait Hut, which is also beautiful but not the right place.

The valley opens out at the top and the track, mercifully,

Red beech (*Nothofagus fusca*) is a key component in the honeydew beech forest of the Rotoiti Nature Recovery Project.

John Sawyer

Jetty at Kerr Bay, departure point for the water-taxi.
Rob Suisted

levels off. By now you'll be surrounded by fantastic scenery, with Mt Angelus on your left. In due course you arrive at the Angelus Hut.

The next day you can return the same way, back down the Cascade Track, and we recommend that you do this if the weather is bad or there are high winds or poor visibility. Otherwise, we suggest a return to St Arnaud via the Robert Ridge, over Flagtop and Mt Robert. This is a longer option but quite spectacular in good weather, and it makes for a magnificent round trip.

You start the route to Mt Robert by following poles from the hut to a steep scree slope, which you climb. This will be a rude awakening after the gourmet meal the night before. The track from here is well marked, taking you along the western side of the ridge and below Julius Summit. Climbing up onto the ridge, the track continues up Flagtop. From here the track drops to the summit of Mt Robert, skirting along the top of the Rainbow skifield. The Pinchgut

Chicken laksa

Laksa is one of the most delicious examples of the mixing of typical Chinese ingredients with Malay herbs, spices and fragrant roots. It is the name for both the noodles and the herb used to flavour the broth. Rich coconut milk is used to make laksa lemak; asam laksa is a sour, tamarind-based version. The term laksa comes from the ancient Persian term for noodles, lakhsha (slippery), brought to the Malay Peninsula by Arab traders around the thirteenth century.

2 tbsp vegetable oil
1½ tbsp laksa paste (e.g. ½ sachet of the Asian
    Home Gourmet brand)
500 ml chicken stock
250 g boneless chicken pieces
100g Nestlé coconut milk powder mixed with
    400 ml water or 1 x 400 ml can coconut milk
½ red capsicum, finely sliced
50 g mung bean sprouts
100 g fine green beans, sliced thinly lengthwise
    (or about 100 g snow peas)
300 g fresh egg noodles (or 120 g dried
    vermicelli)
small handful Vietnamese mint (or regular
    mint), finely chopped
juice of 1 lime
2 spring onions, sliced into 5 cm segments
    (and lengthwise)
¼ cup chopped fresh coriander (or 2 stems,
    leaves removed and chopped)

Vegetarian option
Replace the chicken stock with vegetable stock. Omit the chicken and add 200 g shitake mushrooms and 2 bulbs baby bok choy (quartered).

Heat the oil in a deep pan and sauté the laksa paste over a low heat for a minute until aromatic. Pour in the stock and bring to a simmer. Add the chicken pieces and simmer for about 10 minutes. Add the coconut milk, capsicum, bean sprouts and green beans or snow peas and simmer for another 2–3 minutes or until the vegetables are cooked to your liking.

If using vermicelli noodles, boil some water, remove

it from the heat and soak the noodles in it for 5 minutes. If using fresh egg noodles, add them to the laksa broth and simmer for another 2 minutes. Remove from the heat and stir in the chopped mint and lime juice. If using vermicelli noodles, drain and serve them into two bowl. Pour the laksa over, and top with sliced spring onion and coriander.

Pegaus Bay Riesling (Waipara)

This riesling has aromas and flavours at the citrus end of the spectrum, with lemons, lime and grapefruit elements. These often intermingle with peach, nectarine and a characteristic spice. As it ages, the wine may develop marmalade-like complexities.

Alternative wines

Te Mania Riesling (Nelson)
Huia Gerwürztraminer (Marlborough)

Scarlet mistletoe (*Peraxilla colensoi*) can be seen in glorious flower from October to January in the few places where these climbing plants have not been ravaged by possums.
John Barkla

Track drops steeply away down to the car park. Arrange for a taxi pick-up from here, as it is another seven kilometres back into the village.

The hut

The large hut (36 beds) is on the edge of Lake Angelus. Outside of the main New Zealand holiday periods, it is filled predominantly with overseas trampers. The lake is much bigger than your usual mountain tarn, and surrounded on three sides by a ring of craggy grey mountain ridges.

If you do not want to use the hut, there are some great places to camp nearby, such as beside Hinepuri Tarn, a short walk beyond and down from the hut. However, we recommend the hut: the magnificent view from the kitchen will make your meal taste that much more delicious.

Things to do nearby

An evening walk around Lake Angelus is a good way to relax and stretch your legs. Sandflies can sometimes be a nuisance on the far side of the lake, where there is less wind, so remember to take insect repellent with you. Near the hut in midsummer you will find many interesting flowering native alpine plants, such as *Ourisia, Celmisia* (daisies), speargrass and mats of *Raoulia*.

We recommend you climb Mt Angelus (2,065 metres) but only if you are relatively fit. Take plenty of water with you.

The track along the Robert Ridge involves traversing some steep scree slopes.
C. Rudge, DOC, Crown copyright

Don't bother making this ascent if the weather is clagged in – it is the views from the summit that make this grunt worthwhile. The climb involves descending to Hinapouri Tarn and skirting its northern edge or crossing the stream that leaves the tarn and climbing up the grassy/rocky slopes towards Sunset Saddle. Eventually the vegetation gives way to rocky scree. There are cairns along this part of the track all the way to the saddle, from where it is a 45-minute scramble up loose scree to the summit. There is good cellphone reception from here, so it's a good spot from which to gloat to your friends back at work.

Mt Angelus and the hut beside the lake.
Chris White

General tips

If you have time in St Arnaud, visit DOC's Rotoiti Nature Recovery Project, an integrated pest-management project to protect (with great success) the native forest beside Lake Rotoiti.

There is good fly fishing for brown trout in the Travers River, particularly above the swingbridge and especially before Christmas. You'll need to buy a fishing licence (available from DOC offices).

Welcome Flat Hut

Westland Tai Poutini National Park

6 hours   30 bunks   No
Hard
Summer
NZMS 260 H36 Mt Cook

The southern end of the West Coast is one of the most exhilerating regions in New Zealand, with its unique wilderness, huge beaches, superb views of the country's highest mountains (Aoraki/Mt Cook and Mt Tasman), lakes dotted across the lowlands, and, of course, glaciers.

Time required

A tough tramp for beginners – this takes six to seven hours to the hut, and you'll need extra time if you want to explore the valley above the hut or relax in the hot pools.

The best time to go

Although this tramp can be done year round, a summer trip, from New Year's Eve onwards, is advisable. In spring (and sometimes even in midsummer) avalanches can occur. After heavy rain, which is not uncommon on the West Coast, streams rise rapidly and the many bridges you have to cross may become impassable.

Getting there

The walk in to the Welcome Flat Hut starts at the Copland Track car park, signposted on State Highway 6 beside a bridge over the wide Karangarua River about 30 kilometres south of Fox Glacier village.

If you are crossing the Main Divide from Otago, the drive from Wanaka across the Haast Pass is dramatic. Buses pass the end of the Copland Track every day, going north and south, so there are plenty of options for getting to the starting point of this tramp.

Tramping through bush on the West Coast side of the Copland Track.
John Sawyer

The shopping

Supermarkets in Fox Glacier and Haast will have some provisions, though if you want a wider range at reasonable prices, you should shop in Greymouth or Wanaka.

The tramp

The Welcome Flats tramp is not the easiest prospect, but it is achievable by people of average fitness spurred on by the lure of the hot pools near the hut. Occasionally the track can be washed out, so heed any DOC warnings about stopping in avalanche areas or on the faces of fresh slips.

Setting out from the car park, you immediately have to cross Rough Creek. A 30-minute detour upstream will save you getting your boots wet, but we recommend striding through the water. You'll certainly enjoy a cool soaking on the return trip.

Initially, the track follows the Karangarua River, climbing gently through bush on flats beside the bright blue water before entering a wide forested terrace. A viewpoint over the confluence of the Karangarua and Copland Rivers is worth the two-minute side trip and provides a good opportunity for a scroggin stop.

After a couple of hours the real climb begins as the track bears left to follow the Copland River. You gain height more rapidly now, alternating between bush and riverbed boulders. A number of bridges cross side streams, including McPhee Creek and 'Unnamed Stream'.

A long swingbridge over Architect Creek marks the start of the 300-metre climb to Welcome Flat Hut. The track crosses numerous side streams. If the water levels are too high, there are flood-bridges available just upstream. Along the way you will encounter Palaver Creek, Open Creek and finally, after a steady climb, Shiels Creek.

Just after this is the highest point of the tramp, and from here the final 20 minutes is a descent to the aptly named Welcome Flat through ribbonwood forest. When you see the roof of the hut poking out of trees on the floodplain, you'll certainly experience an immediate sense of achievement (not to mention relief).

A kea perched in flowering southern rata.
Rogan Colbourne, DOC, Crown copyright

Swingbridge on the track up to Welcome Flat.
Emma Riley

Moroccan beef with olive couscous and yoghurt mint sauce

This meal can be eaten a couple of days into a longer tramp, particularly if you marinate the beef beforehand.

Marinade
½ tsp ground cumin
½ tsp ground coriander
½ tsp salt
¼ tsp ground chilli
½ tsp ground ginger
½ tsp fennel seeds
½ tsp paprika
½ tsp ground black pepper
1 tbsp olive oil

380 g beef fillet, cut in two lengthwise

Mix all the spices together and add the olive oil. Lay the two pieces of beef in the marinade and toss to coat the meat. Leave to rest for at least 30 minutes.

Yoghurt sauce
150 ml plain yoghurt
2 tbsp chopped mint
2 tbsp lemon juice
salt and pepper to taste

Again, you can make this sauce before you leave. Mix all the ingredients well and leave to sit for at least 20 minutes.

Olive couscous
2 tbsp olive oil
½ red capsicum, chopped
1 clove garlic, finely chopped
1 small red onion, chopped
100 g couscous
4 tbsp pitted and chopped black olives
4 tbsp flat-leaf parsley, chopped

Heat the olive oil in a saucepan. Add the capsicum and garlic and sauté over a low heat until softened. Add the red onion and sauté for a further 2 minutes. Pour in the couscous and cover with water. Turn off the heat after about a minute. Stir and leave to stand for about 5 minutes. Fluff with a fork and toss the olives and parsley through.

Meanwhile, in a frying pan, heat another 1 tbsp of olive oil until the pan is hot. Sear the beef for about 2 minutes on each of the three sides. Let it rest on a plate for 2–3 minutes. Slice into 1 cm pieces across the grain and serve on top of the olive couscous. Spoon the yoghurt sauce over the top.

2002 Crossroads Talisman (Hawke's Bay)

Talisman is a unique blend of six premium red varieties. After crushing and complete destemming, the individual varietal components were fermented separately in small open-top fermenters, where regular hand-plunging ensured a gentle extraction of the necessary colour and tannin. The young wine was then settled before being racked into French and American oak barriques for 12 months' maturation. The various barrels of wine were progressively blended before being returned to wood for another year. Crossroads' home vineyard is in Fernhill, Hawke's Bay, an area characterised by soils with a high gravel content and low to moderate water retention, resulting in very ripe fruit and full-bodied distinctive wines.

Alternative wine
2002 Red Rock Gravel Pit Red (Hawke's Bay)

John Sawyer at Welcome Flat Hut.
Emma Riley

The hut

This huge hut accommodates 30 in a vast upstairs bunk-room. Downstairs is a large kitchen, but without gas or electricity. This building replaced the original Welcome Flat Hut in 1986, only to be damaged after only 13 weeks by a huge mudslide that swept down the valley. The current location is safe – so they say. It is surrounded by beech forest and only a few minutes' walk from the beautiful Copland River. Views from the region of the hut are magnificent and take in the Sierra Range, including Mt Sefton, and several unnamed glaciers that fill the steep valleys.

Relaxing in a hot pool at Welcome Flat.
Rob Suisted

Things to do nearby

The real reason to hike for six hours uphill into the mountains is not to see fantastic scenery or to eat delicious gourmet food. It is to soak in the natural hot pools that make Welcome Flat one of the most special tramping destinations in New Zealand. The pools were first noted by Charles Douglas in 1896, and have become a haven for weary hikers.

If you have a few spare hours and plenty of energy, we recommend a walk up Welcome Flat to Douglas Rock Hut. The track is easy going as far as Scott Creek, when it starts to climb, crossing open slips and following the steep valley sides of the Copland River. After three hours you will arrive at a swingbridge across Tekano Stream. Immediately after the stream is the hut. About 10–15 minutes further and you reach the treeline, where the huge upper reaches of the Copland Valley open up before you.

The really adventurous can continue over Copland Pass to Aoraki/Mount Cook village, but this is recommended only for well-equipped and experienced alpine trampers.

Douglas Rock Hut, on the way to Copland Pass.
John Sawyer

General tips

In the evening, a bus trip from Fox village will take you to Lake Matheson for one of the most famous short walks in the country, to watch the sunset on the Southern Alps. The lake is only six kilometres down a side road from Fox, and the loop walk around the lake takes only an hour. A series of lookouts give views of the mountains (provided there are no clouds) changing to a salmon-pink colour and, if the wind dies down, you will see a perfect reflection of the mountain chain in the lake.

This is a remarkable experience, so take plenty of film (or card capacity) for your camera.

You cannot visit this part of the world without walking up to the snout of the Fox or Franz Josef Glaciers, or even taking a heli-hike or a guided ice walk on one of the glaciers themselves.

The Copland River and Sierra Range.
John Sawyer

Siberia Hut
Mount Aspiring National Park

2½ hours   20 bunks   No

Easy

February

NZMS 260 F38 Wilkin

Looking up the Siberia Valley.
Les Molloy, DOC, Crown copyright

The Makarora region is a popular destination for people wanting adventure but not the noise and crowds of Queenstown and Wanaka. The jetboat rides are fun and there are many short walks and tramps from small car parks along State Highway 6. A DOC brochure, available from the visitor centre in Makarora, describes these.

Time required
This is a relatively easy two-and-a-half-hour tramp from the water-taxi drop-off point at Kerin Forks. You should allow a few more hours to explore Siberia Valley or, for the energetic, a full day for the return hike to Lake Crucible.

Aboard the jetboat on the Wilkin River to Kerin Forks.
Rob Suisted

The best time to go

The central mountains of Mount Aspiring National Park, west of Makarora, accumulate fantastic amounts of cloud and receive more than their fair share of rain. That means the drier late summer months are the best time to do this tramp. Most of the native plants are in flower from December to January. There are fewer people on this tramp than the more famous Great Walks, but at times you'll have to put up with the 'lazy tourist' flying in by plane or helicopter. You will also have to contend with incontestably annoying sand-flies, but don't let these pests deter you.

Getting there

The starting point for this tramp is Makarora, about half-way between Wanaka and Haast on State Highway 6. Buses pass through daily in both directions, or if you are brave you can hitchhike, as there are large volumes of traffic, especially in summer. From Makarora you will be jetboating up the Wilkin River.

Louisiana jambalaya

Jambalaya is the Cajun–Creole equivalent of paella, though it is more highly spiced than the Spanish dish. Ingredients vary enormously from recipe to recipe, the only constants being rice, tomato, capsicum and onion.

250 g boneless chicken thighs, cut into quarters
2 thick rashers of bacon, cut into chunks
2–3 spiced smoked pork sausages, cut into 1 cm diagonal
    slices
4 tbsp olive oil or 50 g butter
1 small red onion, chopped
1 stick celery, finely chopped
1 clove garlic, chopped
1 small green capsicum, chopped
2 tsp Cajun spice mix (e.g. Paul Prudhomme's Magic
    Seasoning for Chicken)
½ tsp smoked paprika
220 g long-grain rice (about 1 cup)
500 ml chicken stock (or use 2 stock cubes)
2 tomatoes, chopped
1–2 spring onions, chopped (optional)

Sauté the chicken pieces, bacon and sausage in half the olive oil or butter in a frying pan or pot until nicely browned.

Set aside. Add the rest of the oil to a pot and sauté the onion, celery, garlic and capsicum over a medium heat for 3–4 minutes until softened. Add the spice mix and paprika and cook over a low heat for a further minute.

Return the meat to the pan and add the rice, stirring to coat. Tip in all the chicken stock and tomatoes. Stir well and simmer over a low heat with the lid on, stirring occasionally, until the rice is cooked (about 12 minutes). Spoon into bowls and garnish with chopped spring onion if desired.

Carrick Pinot Noir (Central Otago)

Any pinot noir from Central Otago is worth its weight in gold, and the Carrick is no exception. Aromatically it exhibits violets, blackberries and red fruits layered with subtle note of briar and oak. On the palate the fruit flavours are of blackberries, black cherries and red fruits. Carrick do not produce much of this wine, so buy plenty of any vintage to keep for tramps over the next five years or so.

Alternative wine
2002 Kaituna Valley Vineyard Pinot Noir (Awatere)

The giant buttercup *Ranunculus lyallii*.
John Barkla

101

Watch out for tiny rock wren (*Xenicus gilviventris*) on the track to Lake Crucible.
Rod Morris, DOC, Crown copyright

The shopping

Buy all your food before arriving in Makarora, unless you want to survive on ice creams and potato chips. There is a small shop there, but for the gourmet ingredients described below you are best to visit a supermarket in either Wanaka or Haast.

The tramp

After a thrilling ride Wilkin River Jets will drop you off on a grassy bank at Kerin Forks. From here the Siberia Hut track follows the river for a couple of hundred metres into small fragments of beech forest. Then a steady and sometimes steep climb begins up a newly constructed zigzagging path that takes you up onto a ridge, avoiding the deep gorge that drops away to your left. The track levels out after about an hour (or more if you are not very fit). This will help you recover your energy to enjoy the superb views of waterfalls and mountains.

A relaxing descent then leads into the Siberia Valley, along a well-graded path. At first you are in beech forest, but this soon opens up into a flat-bottomed grassy valley. The view up the valley is of Mt Dreadful, on the other side of Siberia Stream (more like a river). In the centre of the valley is the airstrip for 'adventure' flights from Makarora.

The track continues up the valley along a marked track running between the edge of the forest and the stream. After another 40 minutes you arrive at the hut, on the right-hand side and tucked in beneath a steep, forest-clad hillside.

The hut

The hut is excellent, with a veranda from which to enjoy magnificent views up the valley. The only drawback is the sandflies. The kitchen/dining room is huge and there are two bunkrooms, with plenty of places to camp in the valley if you decide the hut is too civilised (or too full).

Things to do nearby

A couple of minutes' walk further up the valley from the hut is a beautiful waterfall with a swimming hole at its base – a perfect spot on a hot summer's day.

If you are feeling more energetic, the three- to four-hour

The white snow marguerite (*Dolichoglottis scorzoneroides*) flowers in January.
John Sawyer

(one way) hike up to Lake Crucible is a must. After about 40 minutes' walk up the valley from the hut on a well-marked track along the flats, the main route bears right into forest for the Wilkin–Young Tramp over Gillespie Pass. At this junction, the Crucible walk turns left to the other side of the valley, crossing Siberia Stream.

This track continues straight up into the forest. You climb for about an hour, cross a small stream and then entering a wide glaciated valley carpeted with native alpine plants (in flower December to January), including the giant *Ranunclus lyallii*. Perched at the head of the valley (and frozen over in winter) is Lake Crucible, formed by glacial action depositing rock to form a huge dam. It is a magnificent sight and well worth the walk. You have to return the same way but will be rewarded with very different views.

Adventurous and fit gourmet trampers may want to continue from Siberia Hut up over Gillespie Saddle (1,570 metres) and down into the Young Valley to complete a superb round trip back to Makarora. This will take another couple of days but is a spectacular route. Crampons and ice axes are required when the pass is covered in snow.

Lake Crucible.
Keith Springer, DOC, Crown copyright

General tips

The enthralling drive across Haast Pass should be included in your travel plans to be undertaken either before or after this gourmet tramp.

Luxmore Hut
Kepler Mountains

3½ hours   56 bunks   Yes

Hard

February

NZMS 260 C43 Manapouri

D43 Te Anau

Luxmore Hut and Lake Te Anau.
John Sawyer

The earliest tracks up onto Mt Luxmore were cut by Jack Beer in the 1890s and early 1900s to provide summer grazing for his sheep. More recently the Kepler Track was built as one of New Zealand's Great Walks and is now one of the country's most popular tramps.

Time required

The tramp to Luxmore Hut takes about three and a half hours from Brod Bay, depending on your fitness level and whether or not you take a water-taxi across Lake Te Anau. If you're up for it, add two hours for the walk from Te Anau township to Brod Bay via the control gates Allow a further two hours if you plan to climb Mt Luxmore before dinner.

Acyphylla crosby-smithii growing near the ridge track to Mt Luxmore.
John Sawyer

The best time to go

The Kepler Mountains are always busy during the summer months, generally with overseas visitors doing the Great Walk. If you don't mind sharing a 60-bed hut with more than 60 people, feel free to join them.

These mountains are very exposed and the weather can turn bad at any time of year. However, the hut is only half an hour's walk from the bushline on the ridge up to Mt Luxmore, so even if there is a lot of snow on the tops you should still be able to make the journey in midwinter.

The DOC visitor centre will advise you on the conditions on the track, and may even close it if the weather is too bad.

South Island edelweiss (*Leucogenes grandiceps*).
John Sawyer

A booking system has been introduced, and in the peak season you must apply for Great Walk hut tickets, which can be obtained at any DOC visitor centre or by emailing greatwalksbookings@doc.govt.nz.

Getting there
This tramp starts in Te Anau, the 'Gateway to Fiordland', at the southern end of the lake. It is an easy drive or bus ride from Invercargill, Dunedin and Queenstown.

The shopping
Te Anau is where you will find many of your provisions. There are plenty of shops, including bakeries, liquor stores, greengrocers and supermarkets. Food is sometimes cheaper in Dunedin and Invercargill, so perhaps shop before you leave if you are travelling from there. The wine options should all be available in Te Anau.

The tramp
Luxmore Hut is a relatively easy walk from Brod Bay (where the water-taxi drops you off) on the Kepler Great Walk. It is not a long tramp, especially if you take a water-taxi from the beach in Te Anau to Brod Bay, which we advise you to do if you are carrying all the food and drink described below. The track is well graded as it climbs 850 metres

The luxurious Luxmore Hut.

John Sawyer

through beech/podocarp forest. The climb sounds considerable but passes quickly and easily. You will have occasional sightings, through beech forest, of Lake Te Anau and beyond. From December to February you may also enjoy glimpses of red-flowering mistletoe in the canopy overhead.

The track skirts the bottom of some huge limestone bluffs and then winds up onto a beech-clad ridge. At the treeline the vegetation breaks quickly to tussock grasses and mountain daisies. The track continues along a wide ridge following cairns. Just as you feel you are about to fall off the edge, you turn a corner and the hut is close at hand.

If you want to do it the hard way, begin your tramp from the DOC visitor centre, at the south of Te Anau. Walk around the lake to the control gates that mark the entrance to the national park and the start of the Kepler Great Walk.

The red-flowered mistletoe *Peraxilla tetrapetala* grows as a hemi-parasite on beech trees.
Owen Spearpoint

The hut

This huge hut was built in 1987, when the Great Walk was constructed. It sleeps 60 in a number of bunkrooms. We advise that you pick the smaller bunkroom at the left-hand end of the hut if you get there in time. The views from the hut of the Murchison Mountains over Lake Te Anau are superb.

On a clear day you might even be able to see a takahe *(Notornis mantelli)* in the bush on the other side of the lake. The rediscovery of this bird, thought to be extinct, in 1948

Takahe (*Notornis mantelli*).
Dave Crouchley, DOC, Crown copyright

Chicken with sun-dried cranberries and mushrooms

8 small potatoes, peeled
140 g green beans
oil or butter for frying
1 large onion, chopped
2 cloves garlic, crushed
3 rashers bacon, diced (use the rest of the packet for breakfast)
150 g large brown flat mushrooms, sliced 1 cm wide
4–6 boneless skinless chicken thighs, each cut into 3 pieces
2 tbsp dried cranberries (or 8 prunes chopped in half)
½ cup red wine (or 1 tsp beef stock with ½ cup water)
1 chicken stock cube with 3 tbsp water
2 tsp sugar
salt and pepper to taste

First, cook the potatoes and beans, and keep them warm while you prepare the chicken. Put the potatoes into a pot of boiling salted water. Cook for 12–14 minutes, then add the beans to the pot and cook for a further 4 minutes.

Drain, remove the beans and mash the potatoes (with some butter if you have any). Set aside.

Sauté the onion, garlic and bacon in oil or butter for a couple of minutes until soft, Add the sliced mushroom and sauté for another couple of minutes.

Add the chicken pieces and cook for a further 2 minutes. Add the cranberries, wine and stock and cook for about 8 minutes. Season with the sugar, salt and pepper.

Serve with the potatoes and beans.

Gibbston Valley Pinot Noir (Central Otago)

Pinot noir is very much at home in Central Otago. The cool continental climate is ideal for this grape variety, and the long, dry, settled autumns allow Gibbston Valley to harvest perfectly ripened fruit with marvellous structure and balance. The attraction is the superb intensity of ripe plums, red berries and cherries. The palate is supported by fine tannins against a background of toasty French oak. This is a fantastic wine that will continue to improve with age.

Alternative wines

Clearview Chardonnay (Hawkes Bay)
Palliser Estate Pinot Noir (Martinborough)

was the reason for the establishment of the Murchison Special Protected Area.

Most significantly, the hut has flush toilets. It is more like a mountain backpackers' lodge than a backcountry hut and should be sponsored by the United Nations, since every night it accommodates people from all over the world. There are gas stoves to cook on, so no need to bring your own.

Things to do nearby

The Luxmore Caves are a 10-minute walk to the south of the hut. You will need to take a torch to explore them and appreciate their stalactite and stalagmite formations. *Chionochloa spiralis* is one of the rarest tussock grasses in New Zealand and grows beside Luxmore Hut – check out this plant in a book before you go so you can recognise it.

If you feel fit, take a snack and a large bottle of water and climb up Mt Luxmore behind the hut. This mountain marks the start of the long ridge walk to Iris Burn (the next stop on the Kepler Great Walk). The hike to the summit should not take more than an hour and, on a clear day, you'll be rewarded with a majestic panorama.

Chionochloa spiralis is a rare grass endemic to Fiordland National Park.
Kelvin lloyd

Luxmore Saddle, on the way to the summit of the mountain.
John Sawyer

General tips

A huge model takahe in the centre of Te Anau township is worth seeing. There are several boat trips available on Lake Te Anau, one of which will take you to see glow-worms on the far side of the lake. While you are in the area you should consider driving the World Heritage Highway to Milford Sound through the Eglinton Valley and taking a cruise out through the fiords to the Tasman Sea.

If you have lots of time, there are plenty of other tramps to do in this vicinity. The DOC visitor centre has all the information you will need.

Mason Bay Hut
Stewart Island/Rakiura

Most of Stewart Island now forms Rakiura National Park, New Zealand's fourteenth and most recently designated. We recommend taking a few extra days to explore the settlements and environs of Oban and Halfmoon Bay.

3 hours   20 bunks   No

Moderate

Summer

NZMS 260 D48, E48, F48

Halfmoon Bay

Time required
This tramp will take three hours from when you are dropped off by the water-taxi, but you will also need plenty of time to explore the dunes and the coast at Mason Bay.

The best time to go
There is a saying in New Zealand: 'If you don't like the weather, just wait a few minutes.' This adage applies to many places throughout the country, and Stewart Island is

Mason Bay, Stewart Island.
Greg Lind, DOC, Crown copyright

The jetty at Freshwater Landing, where the tramp to Mason Bay begins after the water-taxi ride from Golden Bay.
John Sawyer

definitely one of them. It's renowned for having rain every day, but residents are quick to tell you that their annual rainfall is less than Auckland's.

This tramp can be completed year round, but be aware that the weather can change for the worse at any time. It can be very cold in winter and, even in summer, when the wind blows you may wonder why you chose the bottom of New Zealand instead of Fiji for your holiday.

Whenever you visit, expect to see fantastic sunsets. The Maori name for Stewart Island is Rakiura or 'Land of Glowing Skies'. This is a polite way of saying that it is cloudy most of the time, but when the sun sets, the reflections on the water are glorious.

Getting there

This gourmet tramp is on New Zealand's *real* South Island. The capital of Stewart Island is Oban (after its Scottish namesake) and can be reached by fast catamaran (Foveaux Express) from the mainland town of Bluff, or by plane from Invercargill or Dunedin.

You can start the tramp to Mason Bay at Oban, but we assume gourmet trampers will catch a water-taxi from Golden Bay to Freshwater Landing at the western end of Paterson Inlet. (You can also fly in to Mason Bay from Oban and Invercargill, but even we think this is lazy and it will reduce your chance of meeting a wild kiwi on the track.)

The shopping

Shopping can be done on Stewart Island, and we recommend this as a way of supporting local businesses. Prices are not much higher than in supermarkets on the mainland. The main store in Oban has a pretty good wine selection if you have not brought some with you. Some items (such as Puy lentils, red chilli, spinach and perhaps coriander) are best bought in Invercargill. The fish fillets must be acquired at Southern Sea Foods or the Fishermen's Co-op in Oban. If you know what you're doing, have a go at catching your own blue cod. Don't rely on Bluff for anything more than a meal of fish and chips or magnificent fresh oysters in season (March–May).

The tramp

The water-taxi from Golden Bay will drop you off on a small, rickety wharf on the banks of Freshwater Creek. We recommend that you check the tides with the boat operator a few days before you arrive on the island, as access to the drop-off point is possible only at high tide. If you have time it is worth clambering over the swingbridge to have a look at Freshwater Hut and, if you are feeling energetic, leave your bag and climb Rocky Mountain for a great view of the island. Watch out for a New Zealand dotterel (*Charadrius obscurus*), a threatened species, on or near the summit.

Manuka tunnel on the track to Mason Bay.

John Sawyer

The track to Mason Bay is one of New Zealand's most unusual tramps. It starts at the wharf among low scrub along a wide and often boggy path. The land is flat and the only reference point is Rocky Mountain behind you. After a while the track bends and passes over a thick, brown, tannin-rich stream. It is here that the real adventure starts, when the track enters tunnels of manuka. It follows an almost perfectly straight line alongside a long, deep drainage ditch. Tomtits, bellbirds, robins and fantails will come to meet you occasionally and, if you are lucky, you may meet a kiwi.

One of the most memorable parts of the tramp is crossing the Chocolate Swamp. Fortunately, this can now be negotiated on a boardwalk so you don't have to plug slowly through waist-deep mud. Without this you could spend five hours getting to Mason Bay.

Spiced pan-fried blue cod with Puy lentils, wilted spinach and coriander

Puy lentils are named after Le Puy in Auvergne, in the centre of France. They have a fine green skin with steel-blue speckles and have a delicate taste.

1 small onion, finely chopped
2 cloves garlic, finely chopped
1 fresh red chilli, seeded and finely diced (optional),
    or some dried chillies
1 tsp ground coriander
2 tomatoes, chopped
2 tbsp olive oil
180 g Puy lentils (approximately 1 cup)
2½ cups water or chicken stock (or use a chicken stock cube)
zest and juice of 1 lemon
300 g bag spinach, washed (about 2 large handfuls)
300 g blue cod
1 tbsp fresh coriander, chopped

Variations

If you really cannot stomach the thought of lentils, you can mash some potatoes, but lentils do work really well with this. Puy lentils keep their shape and texture nicely. Add some mussels in their shells to the lentils 4 minutes from the end, to open and add their tasty juices to the dish.

Sauté the onion, garlic, chilli, ground coriander and tomatoes in 1 tbsp of the olive oil over a medium heat until the onion softens. Stir in the lentils, pour in the stock and simmer uncovered for about 25 minutes. Add the lemon zest and juice and stir in. Wilt the spinach on top of the lentils for 3–4 minutes.

Panfry the blue cod the rest of the olive oil until cooked through (about 2 minutes each side). Serve the lentils onto two plates, keeping the spinach on top. Arrange the cod on the lentils and sprinkle with fresh coriander.

St Clair Wairau Reserve Sauvignon Blanc (Marlborough)

This wine is a beautiful pale gold colour. The fruit comes from a range of vineyards in the Wairau Valley. It tends to be hugely powerful, with intense, pungent aromas of passion-fruit, blackcurrant and gooseberry. It is full and rich, with well-balanced acidity, and has passionfruit, gooseberry and ripe nettly notes on the palate. Subtle fragrances of honeysuckle add depth to its lingering finish. Whichever vintage you can find, you won't be disappointed.

Alternative wines
Palliser Estate Sauvignon Blanc (Martinborough)
Stoneleigh Riesling (Marlborough)

Pingao (*Desmoscheonus spiralis*), the key sand-binding sedge, on a Mason Bay dune.
John Sawyer

The boardwalk peters out at Little Sand Hill, and from there you walk through flax and rush shrubland on sand dunes with occasional swampy areas. Half an hour after you leave the Chocolate Swamp a turn-off to the right leads to a hunters' cabin and camp.

From here you walk through an old farm and should be able to see the orange roof of the historic homestead in the distance. The area immediately before the house provides your best chance to see kiwi. From here it is a gentle 15-minute walk down through a forest corridor to the hut.

The hut

The recently renovated Mason Bay Hut sleeps 20 and is well laid out. It is tucked neatly into the scrub/forest vegetation about a kilometre inland from the sea. Any nearer and you would never sleep because of the constant booming of the westerly gales that batter the coast, and the huge surf that crashes onto the expansive, arching beach.

If you arrive early, try to get one of the two smaller bunk-rooms at the front. There are no doors separating the rooms, so wherever you are there is no escape from snorers.

The kitchen is separate at the northern end of the hut, with a wood-burning stove and a couple of tables.

Things to do nearby

The most remarkable experience you can have on Stewart Island is an encounter with the endemic Stewart Island kiwi. This usually entails an evening search, although if you are lucky you may meet one during the day. Stewart Island is the only place in the world where kiwi are not totally nocturnal. There are some rules of engagement: signs on the side of the hut indicate what you should *not* do.

We also recommend walking the 10 minutes from the hut down to explore the beach. Listen for the roar of the surf and head in that direction. This is a fabulous place, a vast series of dunes that can be explored in both directions. If you're feeling fit, the short walk up Big Sandhill (156 metres) will allow you to boast about climbing the tallest sandhill in the country. The views are a bonus. The easiest track starts behind the old homestead.

This tramper has had second thoughts about having a swim at Mason Bay.
John Sawyer

Stewart Island kiwi at Mason Bay.
Tui de Roy

General tips

If you don't encounter kiwi on your tramp, take an evening kiwi-spotting tour from the wharf in Halfmoon Bay to Ocean Beach. A half-day trip to Ulva Island Nature Reserve by water-taxi from Golden Bay is also a must, as it gives you an opportunity to see most of Stewart Island's native bird life – including kaka and kakariki – in the wild.

Codfish Island (Whenua Hau) is just across the water from Mason Bay and can be seen from the beach. It is famous for being the home of the rare kakapo, the largest parrot in the world. Kakapo are green parrots that cannot fly, so don't expect them to visit you on Mason Bay beach.

A few extra days on Stewart Island will enable you to sample many of the short walks in the vicinity of Oban, and there is always the South Seas Hotel for a few drinks at day's end.

Weka on Ulva Island.
John Sawyer

Index of recipies